KT-367-853

Emergent Curriculum
in the
Primary Classroom

*Interpreting the Reggio Emilia
Approach in Schools*

CAROL ANNE WIEN
Editor

Teachers College
Columbia University
New York and London

National Association for the
Education of Young Children
Washington, DC

NORWICH CITY COLLEGE		
Stock No.	242882.	
Class	372.19 WIE	
Cat.	B2	Proc	Iw

Published simultaneously by Teachers College Press, 1234 Amsterdam Avenue, New York, NY 10027 and by the National Association for the Education of Young Children, 1313 L Street, N.W., Suite 500, Washington, DC 20005.

Copyright © 2008 by Teachers College, Columbia University

All rights reserved. No part of this publication may be reproduced or transmitted in any form or by any means, electronic or mechanical, including photocopy, or any information storage and retrieval system, without permission from the publisher.

Chapter 4 first appeared as "Learner as Protagonist in a Standardized Curriculum: A Grade Three Unit on the City" in *Canadian Children, 30,* no. 2 (2005), pp. 23–30. Used with permission of the journal of the Canadian Association for Young Children.

The material on "stages" of teacher development of emergent curriculum in Chapter 1 is adapted from a somewhat different version in *Connections, 10,* no. 1 (2006), newsletter of Child Care Connections, Halifax, Nova Scotia. Used with permission.

Figure 11.1 courtesy of Ellen Wright. All other images provided by the contributors.

Library of Congress Cataloging-in-Publication Data

Emergent curriculum in the primary classroom : interpreting the Reggio Emilia approach in schools / Carol Anne Wien, editor.
      p. cm. — (Early childhood education series)
   Includes bibliographical references and index.
    ISBN 978-0-8077-4887-9 (pbk.) — ISBN 978-0-8077-4888-6 (hardcover)
1. Reggio Emilia approach (Early childhood education) 2. Education, Primary—Curricula.
I. Wien, Carol Anne, 1944–
LB1029.R35E44 2008
372.19—dc22   2008002814

ISBN 978-0-8077-4887-9 (paper)
ISBN 978-0-8077-4888-6 (hardcover)

NAEYC item number 2001

Printed on acid-free paper
Manufactured in the United States of America

15 14 13 12 11 10   8 7 6 5 4 3 2

EARLY CHILDHOOD EDUCATION SERIES
Leslie R. Williams, Editor

ADVISORY BOARD: Barbara T. Bowman, Harriet K. Cuffaro, Stephanie Feeney, Doris Pronin Fromberg, Celia Genishi, Stacie G. Goffin, Dominic F. Gullo, Alice Sterling Honig, Elizabeth Jones, Gwen Morgan

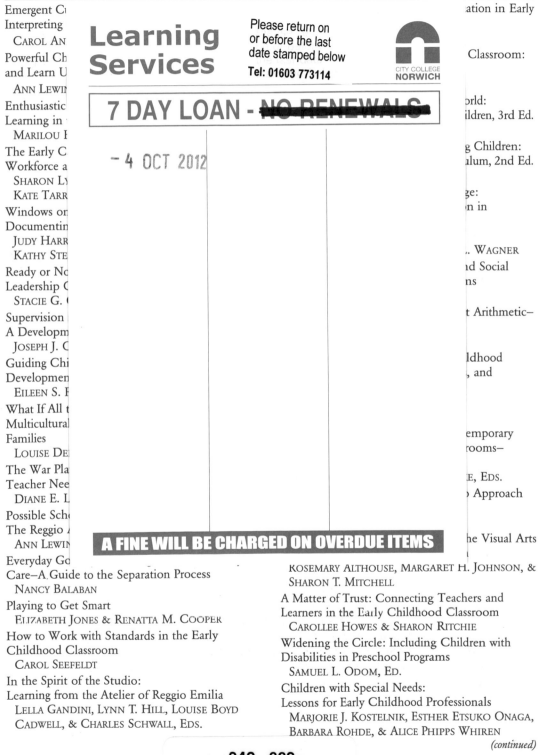

Learning Services

Please return on or before the last date stamped below
Tel: 01603 773114

CITY COLLEGE NORWICH

7 DAY LOAN - ~~NO RENEWALS~~

− 4 OCT 2012

A FINE WILL BE CHARGED ON OVERDUE ITEMS

242 882

for
Fred Wien

Contents

Acknowledgments

We thank the children and their families for the privilege of sharing their vibrant work, their rich thinking and graphic ideas, with others who care about the education of young children. As editor, I cannot help but be grateful to the teachers and principals represented in this collection for their marvelous stamina, their exuberant confidence both in children and in their own capacity to draw wonderful things from them, and the continuous inspiration they give me to carry on in our work together to create more open, participatory, creative spaces within education in which teachers and children might together support each other's learning. The schools too, in their willingness to share the life that goes on within their walls, have our appreciation.

We offer heartfelt gratitude and deep appreciation to the Reggio educators who have so graciously shared their inspirational story over the years. We thank them for the gift of their clarity and for the intellectual, ethical, aesthetic, and affective sophistication of their approach to disseminating their experience. To those we have been able to welcome to Toronto—Carla Rinaldi, Amelia Gambetti, and Lella Gandini—our special thanks for traveling to be with us.

York University, through several deans and associate deans at different times in the Faculty of Education (Stan Shapson and Paul Axelrod, Alice Pitt, Steve Alsop, Steve Gaetz, and Don Dippo), has given me a place in which my thinking and contributions might grow. York has been a gift to me, and my work could not have occurred without it. Part of that gift is also the technical support provided, and I thank Billy Chan for his frequent and patient assistance with computer functioning, especially concerning the images reproduced here.

Teachers College Press has always been, for me, an enjoyable group to work with, and I am again grateful to its editorial team—Marie Ellen Larcada, Wendy Schwartz, David Strauss, Lori Tate, Shannon Waite, and the late Leslie Williams—for all the ways they have helped to build this book.

My debt to specific colleagues but increases with the years: Ann Manicom and Deborah Britzman for sage and warm advice always, Susan Stacey and Barb Bigelow, Laurie Kocher and Pat Tarr, Karyn Callaghan and Jennifer Armstrong, our emergent curriculum group at TDSB—all colleagues who make work a pleasure, a friendship, a collaboration.

My family is the strong foundation upon which all my work is built. I dedicate this book to my husband, Fred Wien, for his gracious patience and ever-willing technical support, for his generosity and tenderness toward all those he mentors, and for his kindness and loving care as my husband.

Introduction

This book highlights exemplary early childhood curriculum for young children in primary classrooms, kindergarten to Grade 3. For a decade, I have watched elementary school teachers take up standardized curriculum in varied ways, from a linear fragmented approach to integrated, participatory, inquiry, and arts-based approaches. Compelling emergent curriculum has been created in schools in spite of the press of standardized curriculum. In *emergent curriculum*, teachers plan in response to the group's interests and concerns, and curriculum expands into genuine inquiry, as children and teachers together become participatory colearners who attempt to understand some aspect of real life. This understanding occurs through multiple ways of learning and creating (in drawing, dance, clay, wire, and so forth) so that new cultures of identity and classroom citizenship develop from it.

The creation of emergent curriculum in elementary public schools, while not a dominant teaching practice, is nonetheless happening in many cities and towns across North America. This book shares examples from one large urban area (Toronto). But we are not unique: emergent curriculum in early childhood education is a grassroots movement among creative, thinking teachers influenced by progressive philosophies. There are pockets of emergent curriculum bubbling up everywhere, like water beginning to boil. This book is for the teachers, administrators, researchers, and policy makers intrigued by emergent curriculum in early childhood education—those who desire insight into it and who hope to nurture and sustain an enlivening, energizing way to learn in classrooms.

As I work with elementary teachers through undergraduate, inservice, and graduate programs in a Faculty of Education, my own inquiry has been to ask how teachers create such wonderful emergent curriculum in schools. How do teachers begin emergent curriculum? How do they sustain it in the face of contrasting pressures? We know it is not an easy or formulaic approach that can be "implemented" like building a deck from a set of plans. Following instructions won't get us there. What are these teachers thinking? What do they believe and value? How do they make decisions about what to do?

In this book, I present nine stories from teachers and principals about their own experiences of emergent curriculum in elementary classrooms. They tell us what they were trying to do, how they went about beginning in the midst of challenges, the decisions they made, their reflections on those moves, and what happened with the children. They directly address questions of standards, for which they feel responsibility. Most of the chapters were developed from theses, research papers, or conference presentations, with the result that the teachers have captured a depth of data and reflection that normally flies by us in the midst of teaching. As mentor to many of the teachers and editor of the collection, I approached these chapters as exemplars that could help us understand how emergent curriculum happens.

I hope to construct a "good-enough" theory of emergent curriculum—good enough as a set of initial reference points for schools that are circumscribed by standardized curriculum and the demand for higher literacy and numeracy scores. Teachers must of course take responsibility for these pressures, and here we see many ways of doing so, and doing much more. This book shows ways an original, creative approach to curriculum design by teachers can be integrated into school classrooms; it also speaks to the inventiveness and commitment of school personnel in keeping alive exciting, challenging, and vibrant forms of teaching practice.

This book also demonstrates the impact of the Reggio Emilia approach to early childhood education on teachers and principals in elementary schools. The Reggio Emilia approach is based in the municipal system of 46 centers for children from birth to age 6, owned and operated by the city of Reggio Emilia in northern Italy since the 1960s. It was initiated by parent cooperatives following World War II and mentored by Loris Malaguzzi from the late 1950s until his death in 1994. The city now has an international center for the study of childhood and maintains ongoing contact, through study tours and conferences, with over 80 countries. All the contributors in this book have studied the Reggio approach; all are teachers who value developmentally appropriate practice and inquiry-based constructivist teaching. They found in the Reggio Emilia approach ways of amplifying and enriching their teaching, even when working in traditional schools. While the Reggio approach has had a vivid impact on early childhood education at the level of child care in many societies worldwide, elementary schooling has been less permeable to outside influences. In this book we see how teachers have made central aspects of Reggio philosophy work in settings where it has been largely unknown and where systemic constraints render any counterpoint to mainstream ways of doing things highly problematic. It shows ways that early childhood values and practices have been sustained and promoted in elementary schools in spite of prevailing forces in policy spheres. It gives hope thus to teachers, families, and children that accountability and efficiency in raising test scores through standardized tests and teaching is not the only form of legitimate teaching and learning in North American cultures of education, and that other forms of progressive education with broader values are alive in public schools.

An additional aspect is the very real concern for building citizenship and understanding of democratic processes that develops in those studying the Reggio Emilia approach. Its history of rising from the ashes of war, of parents insisting their children should be liberated in order to think for themselves, so that they could not again be subjected to fascism, is highly relevant in current environments of less political tolerance of divergent views (Malaguzzi, 1998). Because Reggio Emilia as a city developed a radical, highly progressive, socially democratic form of citizenship with high expectations for citizen participation and responsibility (for example, Carlina Rinaldi, head of the international organization Reggio Children, is also a professor at the local university, as well as a city councilor [Rinaldi,

2006]), its implications for schools as places for democracy suggest radically different ways of systemic functioning than now occurs in many mainstream jurisdictions of public schooling. This book describes situations influenced by Reggio conceptions, from individual teachers altering their classroom structures for the first time to principals and teachers creating more participatory structures among grade teams. Although the book takes curriculum as its focus, it connects with the tradition of examining democracy in schools and highlighting progressive forms of education.

To me, this book is a celebration of really wonderful teaching. In addition to the purposes mentioned, the book also contributes to insights into the importance of positive emotion—individual and collective—in knowledge building. Such positive attachment to learning is a tremendous source of well-being both for classrooms and for individual development, and we know incontrovertibly that emotional well-being and health of the immune system are closely interconnected in the very young (McCain & Mustard, 1999; McCain, Mustard & Shanker, 2007). And how much happier are schools when teachers also have shining eyes and vibrancy! Emergent curriculum makes children want to learn and teachers want to teach.

In summary, the book has five purposes under the broad intention of providing insight into the development of emergent curriculum in schools. It shows stories of exemplary teaching practice for young children. It shows how the influence of the Reggio Emilia approach is reaching into public school environments. It shows examples of democratic participatory teaching that offer visions of responsible citizenship for children. It shares the interrelations of positive attachment, identity, and learning for teachers and children. And it offers a "good-enough" theory of emergent curriculum, describing what teachers are doing to make all this happen so that others might explore such teaching themselves.

THE CONTRIBUTORS

Eight of the nine classrooms described here are in public schools, and one is in an independent nonprofit girls' school. All are in a metropolitan urban area with high immigration from around the world. The classrooms are all diverse, with multiple languages and cultures in each. The contributors are female, some from first- or second-generation immigrant families from places such as Greece, Hong Kong, and South Africa, and some from families that have lived on our continent for more than a century. In addition to teachers, the writers include two principals and an instructional leader; I am especially pleased to have administrators as contributors.

The children and their parents gave permission for the children's ideas, words, photos, plans, and artwork to be shared with others. We use real first names to honor and thank them for their contribution to this book.

The book is organized in two parts, "First Experiences in Emergent Curriculum" and "Long-Term Efforts in Emergent Curriculum." The four chapters in "First Experiences" describe teachers attempting an emergent curriculum, generally for the first time. Nancy Thomas, in Chapter 2, describes how she noticed the children's interest in music, realized it had been occurring a long time in their play, and how she expanded that interest throughout her kindergarten program. In Chapter 3, Shaune Palmer tried her first Reggio-influenced inquiry with a small group of Grade 2 students who were not quite sure their principal could actually be a teacher! In Chapter 4, Noula Berdoussis decided to use the time frame of a unit on the city specified by her standardized curriculum for Grade 3 and, with supportive colleagues in Alice Wong and myself, tried out a very different way of working with the content. In Chapter 5, Deborah Halls invited instructional leader Vanessa Barnett into her kindergarten to explore wire after their visit to the Reggio exhibit "The Hundred Languages of Children."

In the second part, "Long-Term Efforts," the chapters describe contexts of emergent curriculum that lasted 4 to 6 months or with connections across the year in some way. In these longer, more complex pieces, it is more difficult for teachers to describe in detail what they have done over such a time frame, but these writers are all exquisite documenters. In Chapter 6, Susan Hislop reveals her very careful thinking, prodded and probed by her principal, Jennifer Armstrong, and together they show both the limits of children's thinking and children's ingenious problem solving as the first graders tackled mathematical problems through real experience. In Chapter 7, Brenda Jacobs and her hardy group of six kindergarten researchers found a question so difficult for this age group that it astonishes; equally astonishing is the fact that their quest lasted 4 months with great excitement. Noula Berdoussis, in Chapter 8, shows us fascinating moves as a teacher as she led her Grade 1 children from an open playtime, during which they showed an interest in a basket of shells to children theorizing with great interest and excitement about the regeneration of a sea animal. In Chapter 9, Diana Will describes a challenging situation as she attempted to study imagination and inquiry when she had been given the children in Grade 2 with the most difficulties in literacy and numeracy; her description of how she brought a child who was unhappy with school into relationship with inquiry is a revelation. Another revelation is Mary Jane Miller's account of Grade 3 and 4 children's questions about weaving in Chapter 10; what could Kang possibly mean by his astounding question, "Can weaving make a horse?" In Chapter 11, I draw together the key threads that I see in the moves these teachers have made and tease out processes and strategies they used to support emergent curriculum.

In all instances here the children and teachers go far beyond what a standardized curriculum requires and show that humans are more varied, creative, complex, resourceful, and intelligent than such curriculum can ever suggest. It is my belief that emergent curriculum allows teachers, children, and schools to function at the leading edge of their development, showing the highest quality they are capable of, and that witnessing such examples, as we do when reading the chapters here, not only creates a beautiful present, but gives hope for our children's future.

CHAPTER 1

Emergent Curriculum

Carol Anne Wien

The class is so excited: it's like a birthday party in here.
—Grade 1 boy in Noula Berdoussis's class

What do teachers do that gets children so excited they feel that learning is like a birthday party? This book proposes that emergent curriculum wakes up schools and brings teachers, children, and administrators together in collaborative creative processes of learning. The theme that drives this book is the question "What is it that teachers do to create emergent curriculum in elementary schools?" The stories of emergent curriculum in Chapters 2–10 of this book can be read for themselves. In Chapter 11, and in my comments section at the end of each chapter, I attempt to construct a "good-enough" theory of what teachers do to construct occasions of emergent curriculum—good enough as a set of provisional reference points to help us support emergent curriculum now. This chapter offers a general view of the philosophy and practices of the Reggio Emilia approach that have particular meaning for the contributors, a tongue-in-cheek description of teachers' reactions to Reggio-inspired emergent curriculum, and a brief preview of a provisional theory of emergent curriculum. Then we will get right into the stories, which are a delight to read.

Elizabeth Jones and John Nimmo's *Emergent Curriculum* (1994) gave a name to a form of curriculum planning that many constructivist early childhood educators had been pursuing for a generation. While Jones had been using the term since 1970, as Carol Copple notes in her foreword to the book, its title gave the public domain a fresh term for a complex, sophisticated teaching practice, a term that brought into relation the notions of an intentional course to follow, a plan with logic, and its apparent opposite, an emergent or unplanned process. The term *emergent curriculum* thus captures a seeming paradox: an intentional course is implied by the use of the word *curriculum*, derived from the Latin *currere*, meaning to run a course or make one's way around a known route. But paradoxically, the course of this curriculum is not known at the outset. It is emergent—that is, its trajectory develops as a consequence of the logic of the problem, the particular connections that develop as participants bring their own genuine responses to the topic and collaboratively create the course to follow out of these multiple connections. In one of Nancy Thomas's classes, for example, she and her children were walking behind the school next to a vacant lot when they noticed birds dragging their wings. Among old bricks on the ground, a child spotted eggs. This discovery led, in the following weeks, to observation, sketching, camouflage painting, and many literacy and numeracy activities focused on the killdeer and their eggs. We could say that emergent curriculum is building relationships with that which we encounter as we participate with children in knowing the world.

The focus of this book is emergent curriculum inspired by the Reggio Emilia approach. Emergent curriculum has a long tradition in North America, and there are many constructivist approaches to it (e.g., Forman, Lee, Wrisley, & Langley, 1993; Jones, Evans, & Rencken, 2001; Katz & Chard, 2000); the focus in this book is teachers in elementary schools coming to emergent curriculum through their study of the Reggio Emilia approach. The Reggio Emilia approach is neither a model to copy nor a program to implement: "Reggio schools are in Reggio Emilia" (Gambetti & Gandini, 2006). What Reggio Emilia as a region has created in its pre-schools for early childhood education is specific to the cultural context, language, history, geography, and political and economic life of the place and its people. When we are inspired by what they have accomplished and try out a different practice (different to us) in our own cultures of schooling, we are not creating a Reggio approach in schools. We are working with the ideas and philosophies of Reggio Emilia as catalysts to rethinking our own practices. We are re-creating our own teaching and learning practices, using their ideas and practices as reference points and creating our own interpretations of these in our schools. What we create here may not look at all like what we would see in Reggio Emilia, but is our own creation of practices new to us. As the Reggio Children organization consistently argues, what we are creating is an interpretation that fits our own culture, language, place, and time (e.g., Spaggiari, cited in Cadwell, 2003). What we share in the chapters of this book is not "Reggio in schools" but newly created teaching practice, developed when specific Reggio ideas were interpreted to mesh with our own cultures of schooling. In my view, the term *emergent curriculum* best suits these newly created practices of teaching and learning.

THE CONTRIBUTION OF THE REGGIO EMILIA APPROACH

The keystone in the Reggio philosophy, in terms of its impact as an inspiration to the contributors of this book, is the image of children *and teachers* as capable, resourceful, powerful protagonists of their own experience (Malaguzzi, 1998; Rinaldi, 1998). This image in itself invites us to consider standardized, prescriptive, canned, and "teacher-proof" programs inadequate to the creative potential in children and teachers. What does the Reggio image of capability mean for curriculum and program design?

Expansive Values

Three consequences of this central image are expansive values that emphasize relationality, reciprocity, and collaboration in all learning situations.

Relationality. Relationality includes two broad conceptualizations for this book. It includes relationship building among people, but equally so it includes the notion of supporting children and teachers in grasping the interconnectiveness of all living things and our responsibility to sustain life. In this latter sense the philosophy of relationality is linked with complexity theory, the study of non-linear dynamic systems (Bateson, 1979; Davis & Sumara, 1997; Poerksen, 2004). To emphasize relationality means to de-emphasize evaluation and measurement and to think more broadly of how one system affects another in interrelated systems of dynamic change.

Reciprocity. A second consequence of the image of children and teachers as capable and resourceful is an emphasis on reciprocity. Reciprocity is mutual exchange, that is, a sharing of power with living things that allows room for all to be included and each to have a voice. Reciprocity speaks to spaces for participation and to responsiveness on the part of teachers. In prescriptive programs, reciprocity is ruled out by design (Franklin, 1999; Wien, 2004b).

Collaboration. A third emphasis is collaboration, a set of social processes growing out of Reggio Emilia's peculiar relationship with socialism, which we interpret as emphasizing a more collective rather than individualized vision of life together, and a strong sense of participating in a social democracy. Such a vision of collaboration asks for more integrated participation and responsibility from citizens.

Expansive Ideas

In addition, there are three other big ideas from the Reggio experience that have had particular influence on the contributors to this book and that continue to goad us to rethink our teaching practice in schools further.

Organic metaphors. In Reggio articles and presentations for study tours, we find the use of organic metaphors for education rather than the more common mechanistic metaphors of education used widely in mainstream North American education. The most common metaphor is of education as a machine related to industrialization. Rather than speaking of inputs, outputs, productivity, and the language of economic production, however, Reggio speaks of "school as a living organism" (Malaguzzi, 1998). It is a radical shift in thinking to conceive of schools as interconnected living systems that require sustenance, nurturing, room to move, grow, and house the pulse of life, instead of as institutions for the production of knowledge based in bureaucratic processes of regulation. How does this view change our conceptions of schools? Recent descriptions of how biologists now think of defining life (e.g., Capra, 2002) argue that living organisms have a boundary that holds the system together, but a permeable boundary through which matter flows in and out. In addition, a living system is capable of responding within its environment in ways that are open and creative, not predetermined. To use a metaphor of school as a living system with permeable boundaries and adaptivity opens our thinking to a startlingly different conception of ways of doing things and assessing the results.

Children as citizens. A second major idea is the emphasis on children as citizens with rights to participate in society, according to their level of development. To speak of infants as having rights to a social experience, as we were told in the 2002 study tour, or children with "special rights" (versus our terminology of special needs for special education) puts the onus on adult responsibility to provide adequate resources that permit full participation of the most vulnerable members of Reggian society. This value of participation is seen throughout their system (Rinaldi, 2001), for example in the sharing of children's and teachers' responses to the abstract artist Alberto Burri's work in *Children, Art, Artists* (Vecchi & Giudici, 2004).

Children as creators of culture. Related to the notion of children having rights to participate in society, a third major idea is the emphasis on children's right to contribute their creative inventions and designs to the life of the culture around them. This emphasis sees children not merely as consumers of mass culture, as promoted to children through mass media advertising and technology, but values children as creative participants in the work of design and invention that contributes to their society. This right to contribute to the culture of their city and region gives young children a place of belonging and identity in the culture that creates attachment to life, to place, to responsibility. Anyone familiar with Reggio work will have favorite examples of these creations. Most would recognize as supreme examples the fountains created by Giovanni Piazza, children, and parents of La Villeta School for *An Amusement Park for Birds* (Forman & Gandini, 1994), which still function over a decade after their construction, and Vecchi's work with children to create, in quarter scale, the design for a new theater curtain (Vecchi, 2002). Such accomplishments show us the distance between our own values and those of Reggio schools, for these creations seem audacious from our vantage points, yet also related to the spirit of innovation and design so valued by our society. We look at what Reggio children have done and believe we could do so much more with our own children!

These big values—relationality, reciprocity, collaboration—and these big ideas—children as rich protagonists of experience, school as a living organism, children's right to participate in society, children's right to be creators of culture in addition to consumers—form an overarching framework (Schon, 1983) for the practice of teaching and learning that has helped shape the work of the teachers in this book. We asked what it would mean to take some of these ideas seriously in our own classrooms and schools. However, we would have little idea of how the city of Reggio Emilia has created such accomplished schools without their ardent willingness to disseminate their work, and their vibrant attempts to share what they are doing in the interests of exchange with other educators around the world.

Expansive Practices

In this sharing, the educators of Reggio Emilia have also introduced us to classroom practices of teaching and learning that take us further than we knew was possible. Four of these practices are particularly pertinent to this book: The notion of the environment as a third teacher, pedagogical documentation, the "hundred languages of learning," and "progettazione." [This description is not, of course, a comprehensive or exhaustive explication of their ideas—it is a recognition of those practices that had the most influence on the contexts of this book.]

The environment as a third teacher. This notion speaks to the capacity of the environment to engage and shape learning interactions. Space and its objects-in-relation can be organized, designed, layered, and bounded in ways that invite learning without teacher intervention. Many teachers in elementary classrooms are accustomed to complex *time* schedules as organizers for what to do, but are less attuned to ways that organization of *space* effects learning. Teachers with early childhood background or with Montessori training with its notion of the prepared environment have stronger notions of the impact of spatial design of the environment on learning.

Here is a story from Reggio experience to describe the environment as a third teacher (see also Wien, 1997). During the 1997 American study tour, in the Diana school between the inside of the atelier and the playground outside, that is, just in the doorway on the patio threshold, teachers whom we did not meet (they were away at a conference) placed a large low table that drew our eyes immediately as we headed outdoors where children played. The large low table was full of a vast array of natural plant items organized in transparent containers—pink and magenta and orange petals, seeds, tiny grasses, and leaves. There was a bouquet of poppies and May wildflowers in a vase, and a stack of platter-size leaves. We recognized the makings of dry nature collages but who were they for? It was beautiful, inviting, and created a bridge between indoors and outdoors—contents from the outdoors mediated by teacher organization. With no teacher in sight it opened an interactive space. What happened? As we stood around admiring, a lively girl picked a poppy bud, took up a dark green leaf platter, and spread the bud open on it. An adult visitor added pink petals, and soon children and adults were making collage arrangements together, smiling, gesturing, reacting to choices of petals or seeds with animated facial expressions. We could not speak Italian, but it did not matter, for the table of organized materials carried the interaction forward, as the children invited us to participate with them and together we had a wonderful time playing with these beautiful natural materials. This to me is an example of the environment as a third teacher, a space organized for particular learning possibilities by its placement, design, and content. It brought children and foreign visitors together to interact in relational ways; if we had merely stood on the edge of the playground looking at children this relationality would likely not have occurred, or might have been momentary instead of a prolonged engagement. In this book, Chapter 2 by Nancy Thomas shows aspects of how environment shaped responses, acting as a "teacher."

Pedagogical documentation. This phrase was initiated by Dahlberg, Moss, and Pence (1999) to distinguish this specialized form of classroom teacher research from other forms of documentation in schools. On the surface, such pedagogical documentation appears to be a presentation of what children are doing, thinking, and feeling in school, presented in visual and text forms (photographs, children's words, sample work, teachers' explanations). But pedagogical documentation, as this book interprets it, is not merely about recounts of what children have done, although when North American teachers first try this complex process, recounts are what they tend to produce. Because they must first develop habits of using the tools of documentation, their focus is on getting those habits in place, and it is difficult at that stage to see further than recounts of experience. But once the habits of documenting are in place—observing children closely, taking photographs, studying the work that children generate, preparing these materials to share with children and others—then teachers in schools can take their documentation further into attempting to make children's thinking, their theories about the world, visible to others. The notion of making learning visible, explicitly visible, requires teachers to examine their notions of learning, and to evaluate their planning and decision making. The construction of pedagogical documentation to share with others is as demanding as writing an academic paper, for the teachers must decide upon their focus, select data from their ethnographic materials that fit their focus, analyze what has happened in terms of teaching and learning, and prepare a layout that communicates to others. But developing pedagogical documentation is merely the beginning.

This book promotes the interpretation that pedagogical documentation is a form of conscious teacher research. Teachers have consciously chosen to inquire into some aspect of children's understanding about the world and some ways of showing their thinking and then attempt to make this visible and communicable to others. This content can be taken up as a subject of study among teachers, parents, and children and investigated for the various interpretations the audience finds in it. Such close study becomes content that affects planning and decision making about what to teach, what to design for learning. Thus pedagogical documentation is both a methodology of teacher research to make children's thinking and learning visible and interpretable to others, *and* a methodology for planning emergent curriculum. Content emerges through studying pedagogical documentation. When teachers revisit documentation with children, it has effects that drive curriculum forward. Some of the more sophisticated effects of pedagogical documentation are seen in Chapter 8 by Noula Berdoussis and Chapter 10 by Mary Jane Miller.

The *"hundred languages of learning."* While we in North America are widely reminded of the importance of using various modes of learning to reach all learners, such as theories of multiple intelligences or brain-based learning or arts-based inquiry (e.g., Caine & Caine, 1997; Eisner, 1997; Gardner, 1999), Reggio educators have widened our horizons about possible new worlds of materials and modes of learning to consider in educating young children. Few of us had thought to use light as an element of curriculum; the introduction of light tables, overhead projectors, and shadow screens to explore light, shadow, color, form, transparency, and so forth was a revelation to most of us and led us to consider a much wider range of potential materials for use in schools. Wire is another material seldom explored in our contexts and opens us to a language of expression with possibilities we never dreamt. Most chapters in this book show teachers and principals expanding their use of materials beyond what we might think typical in schools, and Vanessa Barnett and Deborah Halls's work in Chapter 5 is the first exploration we have seen of wire in kindergarten in our area. It is intriguing to consider the effects of opening our conceptions of usable materials and modes of learning.

In addition, the Reggio conception of conversation as a language of learning, a route to intersubjectivity, and the attunedness required in a group to grasp what someone else is thinking, has offered us a different use of talk than we customarily hear in schools. Then the interconnections between talking in order to think and creating with materials in order to think propels learning further than we expected. We see this propulsion from interconnections among languages of learning especially in Chapters 8, 9, and 10.

"Progettazione." I value the Reggio educators' insistence that this term does not translate well into English, that its meanings are never quite captured, though it means literally "projecting ahead." In this book, we use Malaguzzi's notion of "reconnaissance" as a guide to grasping new ideas about planning suggested by the term *progettazione*. We do not know whether our sense of the term *reconnaissance* connects precisely with Malaguzzi's meaning, but to the contributors in this book, it means a kind of scouting of the wide learning landscape to hypothesize possible routes that the children's thinking and interests might take, and a preparedness to support that interest and to scaffold it to accomplishment by using many means. It means keeping in mind not a single plan for a unit to be followed like a pathway, but a sense of multiple possibilities and multiple routes to knowing, and many ways that teachers and children might together choose. Out of the multiplicity considered—ideally in collaboration with others—the routes chosen reciprocate the particularities of the learning context that arose. Teachers' responses, provisions of materials, and provocations and invitations can thus be highly original as they are matched exactly to the conditions developed by the routes of the children's learning.

STAGES IN TEACHER DEVELOPMENT OF EMERGENT CURRICULUM

To provide a bridge between the general description of Reggio philosophy and practices and teachers' work with it in the chapters that follow, I include here a summary of the sorts of reactions that I find teachers have to ideas of emergent curriculum at different points of engagement with it. I hypothesize four stages in their understanding and habits of emergent curriculum: the challenged teacher, the novice teacher, the practicing teacher, and the master teacher. I describe these stages through the device of imaginary conversations, conflations of many conversations of the sort I have with teachers as we work together, so what follows is a version of emergent curriculum that takes us into the lives of teachers in schools (adapted from Wien, 2006). The contributors in this book range from novices to master teachers, for one school is fully Reggio-inspired throughout its primary division.

The Challenged Teacher of Emergent Curriculum

"I like the idea of emergent curriculum but I don't seem to be doing it. I don't know how to do this. What do children's interests look like anyway? They seem to fly by in an instant. I'm supposed to be teaching literacy and numeracy. What would I do if I found an interest in the midst of all the expectations I have to cover? What should I do that's different from what I normally do—like rotating them through activity centers or letting them play while I do reading conferences? Yet I'm amazed at what the Reggio children can do. Why can't my children do that?"

The Novice Teacher of Emergent Curriculum

"Ah, there, I made something work for a moment. Caught the excitement. What did I do that was different? Was it the conversation? Not having an answer in mind that they should give me? My enthusiastic response to their ideas? Why am I documenting? I either can't seem to do it or I can do some photos with captions. It just seems to me I'm making more work for myself when I should be assessing reading levels. What am I supposed to do with all these photos? I can't find time for it anyway. Although the children do love looking at themselves and talking about what they were doing. And parents like it, if they come in the classroom. It does spark conversation in a different way—not about levels and scores. Parents seem less stressed, more interested. Actually, me too."

The Practicing Teacher of Emergent Curriculum

"Yes, I grasp how to have a conversation with children that gets at their ideas and theories. I know how to take an idea or theory and make it visible through documentation for children and parents, but there's so much going on I hardly know where to turn. I can't keep up with it. I get bits of documentation done but there's so much that intervenes—the toilet overflowed, and five children have lice, and there's no assistant for my special needs child, it's just endless—and all those are part of our living together in schools too. And it's so hard to find colleagues to share and study the work together, yet I know that's so necessary. But three of us meet a couple of times a month, and our VP is impressed at what's happening in our rooms. I observe our environment constantly to assess how it shapes the children's behavior and whether I can correct something that isn't functioning well by altering the environment. I assess materials, quantity of them and numbers of choices available, whether to reroute traffic paths, whether sound quality is a problem, whether the time frames give them enough room to explore and discover at their pace. I still do some things in more traditional ways, math especially, and we have more interruptions than I like, but I do have a long block of time each day for a great variety of rich, integrated processes that involve many 'languages of learning,' many ways of doing things."

The Master Teacher of Emergent Curriculum

"We do all the things the practicing teacher does—careful documentation that pushes our own understanding and study, working with our own inquiries into children's learning, checking our understanding against both what we see in the children and what we are reading about. I have a sense of being part of a team; we work collaboratively, bouncing our understandings off each other and enjoying different interpretations that widen our thinking. We enjoy predicting what the children will do and figuring out various directions in which thinking and action might move. We try to prepare for those, to have materials at hand. My documenting habits are secure. I don't document everything, I decide really carefully what to document, and it's connected to what we're studying. We decide beforehand who will use the camera and take notes, and we talk about it afterwards. Of course, I can only do this really well when I have a student teacher or instructional leader around; otherwise I have to wait to chat with the grade team. But we are in and out of each other's classrooms all the time. We work with the environment a lot, and the organization of time, keeping it open. We go out into the community and bring visitors in. We are conscious of layering many things into the day—conversations, many modes of expression like clay or dance or wire work, keeping parents involved—many, many layers. I find I can sense possibilities in the children, and find ways to draw them out so we can work with them, expand them."

TOWARD A "GOOD-ENOUGH" THEORY OF EMERGENT CURRICULUM

When we attempt emergent curriculum in classrooms, we immediately find it is more difficult than we expected; it doesn't happen just because we want it to. It is more troubling, uncertain, anxiety-producing. But then we notice that we feel fully alive, bursting with higher, positive energy that feels like life itself. If traditional teaching can feel like a rehearsal—like waiting to live one's life—both for children and teachers, then emergent curriculum is living life at full throttle. Teachers say it is so exciting that it is like being on vacation every day, or so exciting you can taste it when you enter a classroom (Wien, 2004a). To understand it better might lend emergent curriculum more legitimacy in elementary schools where teachers are so subjected to prescriptive processes and the exhaustion and deadening of spirit that accrues from living them out (Wien, 2004b).

A FRAMEWORK OF FIVE

As a provisional framework for the "good-enough" theory, I set out five aspects of emergent curriculum below, and I will return to them in Chapter 11 and see how they hold. For each of these five, I find that the language we use can be compared with the language we have learned from the Reggio Emilia approach. However, the connections we make are our interpretation, for we can never know that the meaning of words to us in English matches the meaning Italian words have for Reggio educators. Thus we make a connection useful to us, but recognize that this is our interpretation and that Reggio educators might find themselves surprised by our meaning. Our understanding is circumscribed by our own cultural lens and we must accept that our cultural perspective may be different from theirs. I align Reggio notions of a pedagogy of listening with our traditions of classroom teacher research. This teacher research is carried out via the vehicle of pedagogical documentation, which bears close resemblance to our ethnographic methodologies with the addition of visual aspects. I align democratic or participatory structures with the Reggio notion of children and teachers as rich protagonists of their own experience. I align self-regulating groups with Reggio discussions of collaboration, although I believe collaboration has very different meanings for them than it has for us (Wien, 2000). I align design work and creativity with the Reggio notion of a "hundred languages of learning." Lastly, I borrow from a Buddhist tradition to articulate an effect of emergent curriculum essential to why it is important for schools, an effect that has made Reggio a magnet for attention to young children the world over.

Teacher Research

Research, or looking again, is also a kind of listening. Listening carries the meaning of intersubjectivity, that is, attempting to understand what someone else has in mind (Bruner, 1996). What does this person think, feel, value? Can we grasp their thinking? Their feeling? Listening starts with the adult trying to grasp the children's perspective and build from there, rather than starting with curriculum content. If teachers are trying to understand, they are also studying, researching and learning in response to what they are investigating. In emergent curriculum there is the sense that teachers learn as much as children, through their own active inquiries into children's learning and meaning making.

Participatory Structures of Democracy

A group takes action through shared activity, a context in which each member has an equal voice. In emergent curriculum there is a sense of children and teachers as protagonists of their own experience. There is group ownership of planning and decision making about what to do. It is a collaboration among teachers and children in which the teacher sustains an envelope of safety within which the children may take action. Within this envelope of safety exist multiple degrees of freedom for children to choose their activity. High degrees of freedom to choose what to do are necessary to participation in society.

Discipline of Self-Regulating Groups

Through developing and taking action together, the group develops a self-regulation, a sense of how to be in the group for this learning process, this play episode, how to sustain itself around the topic, how to concentrate. Exploring the topic together with a shared purpose leads to group self-discipline. Because of this self-discipline within the curriculum, teachers find that traditional discipline as correction or holding children to the task is not necessary. I conceive of this self-discipline as ownership by the group of the curriculum, and knowledge of how to work in the group growing out of that ownership. The group has set its own implicit boundaries of containment and lives within them.

Creativity of Design Work

The creative process always involves an inquiry or quest—something un-known—that drives participants on a search (or journey) to find, design, or create a satisfactory solution (Wallas, 1926). It may be a search to find or understand something, as in the quest of scientists, or to make something, as in the quest of an artist, musician, tool maker, dancer, chef, gardener, and so forth. Creativity is par-ticular to the context of a problem and becomes original because local contexts are diverse and individual children unique. When we visit Reggio schools we see cre-ations that children have made for succeeding generations of children—working fountains, or Georgia's weeping fountain resting under a glass table, or play spac-es of embroidered skies made with blue net and silk thread, and wire sculpture clouds. These creations stay as permanent contributions in the school. The creative "little room" inside young children (Beattie in Wien & Callaghan, 2007) has found a place of identity in the external world. To find this creative identity, both inside and outside the self, at age 5 or 6, is a powerful positive anchor of attachment to life. The windhorse effect described next comes in part from creative processes that learners engage in when thinking up their own questions and finding their own routes to provisional answers.

Windhorse Effect

The term *windhorse* is borrowed from the secular Buddhist tradition called Shambhala (Trungpa, 1987) and refers to raising positive energy, the life force that whirls through us. I use it here to refer to the animation by emotion that occurs in emergent curriculum, the sense of feeling as an electric current that excites every-one involved and enlivens programs. This positive energy draws others in around it—parents, visitors—creating larger circles of positive energy that spin out into the community. It is initially a by-product of creative activity and then a kind of fuel for further learning and activity. It suggests parallels with the mental state described in flow theory (Csikszentmihalyi, 1990). As in flow theory, we can hy-pothesize that in emergent curriculum a different mental state develops for those collaborating together on a project, and this altered intention, motivation, and en-ergy carries individuals or the group in the way that the metaphor "windhorse" suggests—the energy has the power of a horse carrying the rider at great speed. This concept does not lend itself to traditional academic definitions or references, yet I believe it is a central aspect of emergent curriculum. If we do not recognize it, we omit an essential feature of emergent curriculum and one of its most positive aspects for schooling. I believe it is this tremendous energy sweeping through the group and propelling its learning that has profound effects for children's develop-ment. For one thing, it is the things we feel most strongly that are remembered. Learning contexts with a penumbra of strong emotion around them have a chance of being remembered. Since humans tend to forget what is not necessary to func-tioning (Norretranders, 1998), such vivid and positive experience contributes to shaping children's identity as learners and teachers' identity as teachers. As we watch the organization Reggio Children build an international center for child-hood culture to accommodate frequent study tours from over 80 countries, we wit-ness the windhorse effect reaching worldwide to draw in excited students of the Reggio Emilia approach, intent on creating some of the same great positive surge in their own cultures of schooling.

Emergent curriculum centers itself in the genuine interest of children and teachers. In other words, it puts the value of motivation—integrity of feeling—first. It says in effect, that education—a leading out—and learning cannot occur without the engagement of both teacher and learner. How is such motivation guaranteed? It is guaranteed by the fact that we are always interested in our own questions and in our own ideas. If we permit children and teachers to engage with their own questions, their own theories about how things work, and their own processes for making things happen and understanding the world, then we can guarantee inter-est and motivation. Motivation fuels learning; it is the positive energy that carries the learner through the curriculum. At its best, learning is effortless and inspired because the energy from motivation is so powerful that it carries the will.

As we read the chapters that follow, we can ask behind the scenes, what is it that teachers do to coconstruct and create emergent curriculum with the children in their classroom? It is easy enough to describe in general terms, as I did ear-lier, but what range of moves, skills and capacities, sensitivities and sensibilities does a teacher who works in emergent curriculum encompass, and what values—ethical, educational, developmental, cultural—inform the choices among moves that teachers make? What degrees of freedom does the teacher entertain, both for the children and for herself? And most significantly, since emergent curriculum is often marked by the uncertainty of the unknown, what does she choose to do when she does not know what to do? How does she gently work her way through the "cognitive knot," as the Reggio educators say, of not knowing how to proceed (Rinaldi, 1998)? And how does she convince others—such as parents, administra-tors, and her own colleagues—that she is a competent member of the profession of teachers, when she does not know how to proceed?

FIRST EXPERIENCES
IN EMERGENT CURRICULUM

CHAPTER 2

Small Boxes, Big Sounds
Spontaneous Music in Kindergarten

Nancy Thomas

Small boxes, taped and glued together, containing pasta and other tiny things, often appeared at music time. I teach kindergarten in a highly diverse school in an area with many new immigrants to Canada. It is a mixed-age kindergarten with 3-, 4-, and 5-year-olds in a classroom set up with multiple areas for activity. The classroom, though small in size, is huge in opportunities for the children through activity centers. These include areas for painting, collage, drawing, writing, drama, and blocks; a snack table; areas for math manipulatives and science; a sand and water play area; and a book corner. I also have no problem using the hall as an extension of our classroom and, in fact, the bulletin board in the hall across from our doorway displays children's work, inviting teachers, parents, and visitors to share in our learning. My main purpose as children start school is to support children in all aspects of their learning (social, cognitive, emotional, physical) and encourage them to become independent while also contributing to the community interdependence of the classroom. I see them as lifelong learners and consider inquiry important: I want them to question and disobey, if necessary!

In May I realized that one or more children would arrive at our final meeting of the day with "instruments" that they had made. The meeting is a time for recapping the afternoon and singing some songs together. These children would bring their little boxes with pasta, bread tags, or bottle caps inside to shake while we played CDs and sang in our music circle. Sometimes I observed children scurrying to the collage table when our tidy-up song, "Jelly Man Kelly," started, and quickly grabbing a small toothpaste box or soap box, dipping their hand into the pasta bin and putting the bits inside, quickly taping the box shut, and then shaking it in time to the music as we sang. Other instruments were more elaborate, with designs, stickers, or colored ribbons attached and very heavily taped—secure as a Brinks truck. I began to wonder whether the children might be interested in learning more about musical instruments. I realized children had been making these instrument shakers for a long time, maybe two months, but sometimes the children's interest has to hit me like a cement block, and that in itself is a testimony to their persistence.

Kathy Scott, a York University teacher candidate, had been in the classroom 2 days a week since January, and we looked forward to her full-time block in May.

When Kathy and I discussed her plan for this 3-week teaching block, it seemed a perfect opportunity to focus on this ongoing interest of the children in musical instruments and their sounds. I felt it was important for Kathy to focus on a real interest of the children because that is where "enduring learning" really occurs (Wiggins & McTighe, 1998). I wanted her to see that the paper curriculum (Ministry of Education and Training, 1998a) could be "covered" by being embedded in a child-centered classroom. I wanted her to experience the joy and excitement of living in a classroom where the teacher is learning as much as the children. And for my own puposes, I wanted to pursue this inquiry when I could collaborate and plan with someone else. Kathy wanted her teaching block to be a time of exploration, curiosity, and wonder, not a series of rote learning, for she had been taught that curriculum should begin with children's interests. Although both Kathy and I enjoy music and love singing with the children, neither of us feels that music is one of our teaching strengths. Thus it struck us as a worthwhile focus also because it was an interesting area for us to explore as colearners with the children. We would have to rely on the expertise of our colleagues on staff at school and on parents and friends to help us.

BRINGING MUSIC INTO THE CLASSROOM

Visitors with Instruments

During Kathy's teaching block in May, we invited visitors with instruments to come to class. A father came with his electric guitar, and a fellow teacher brought his saxophone. They played for the children and showed the important parts of their instruments and how the sound was produced. The saxophone player invited children to conduct, using a hand position high or low in the air, and he responded with high or low notes. The children loved this and laughed in sheer delight when quick hand movements resulted in "funny" sounds, as the pitch rode up and down until the player's cheeks were exhausted.

Playing Musician

During the time when visitors were coming with different instruments to play, Kathy also brought some real instruments into our classroom—a guitar, snare drums, and harmonica, for instance. Kathy said: "Our classroom had a set of plastic instruments, but I felt it was important for the children to touch, see, feel, and use real instruments. Children's faces lit up when they heard a sound from a real instrument. They treated my instruments with great respect. They were curious about the different components of each instrument (tuning keys, fret board, reed, and so forth). They made a sign up sheet that turned out to be a mile long just to have time with the instruments."

I was surprised at the respect and care the children displayed when handling the real instruments. I was reminded of Reggio Emilia and how they provide "real stuff" for the children. I remembered a slide from the *Open Window* set where a boy is playing the drums (Reggio Children, 1993). In our class, Sarbjot, whose mother

FIGURE 2.1. Nancy was impressed by how naturally Sarbjot held the guitar.

said he had never held a guitar before, held it in such a careful, respectful manner: It seemed to be a part of him and I am astonished by his intuitive expertise (see Figure 2.1). Some children were fascinated by the guitar's pick, asking to see it, hold it, wondering what it was for. Some even made their own picks to try out. Others paid close attention to the strings on the guitar, noticing the thick and thin strings, the gold and silver colors.

Our big block area on the carpet was often transformed into a stage for musical performers. There were three or four boys who usually built the stage each day, laying the blocks out side by side in a 10′ x 12′ area. Sometimes they built a riser on top of this platform. We could not leave the stage up each day because our classroom is so small that this is the meeting area for discussions, story reading, and our book center. I had added a microphone—real, but not hooked up. There were two girls in particular who liked to use the microphone and sing and perform on the stage. One child's performances were similar to the *Much Music* channel on TV, and the other's were more "classy" in a Diana Krall tradition—she cruised around the room with mike in hand. I wondered whether it was a gender thing that the boys were building the stage and girls were performing.

Observational Drawing

We decided to set up a sketching area with real instruments so the children could explore with their eyes and hands in more detail and depth, by slowing down to look carefully, exactly what is present and visible in each instrument physically. As they noticed these elements, they might also think about how each part helps make the sound the instrument produces. Or they might not, but the possibility of exploring the relationship between parts—for instance, guitar string and sound box—requires perceptual precision when the child tries to draw how these are connected (see Figure 2.2). For instance, Sarbjot's drawing appears to have three strings, and Rayanna's has eight, or possibly six if the two outermost lines are the outside edges of the fret board. It's hard to tell. But it is amazing to me how much the sketches reveal about what the children see as significant and can articulate on paper.

Experimenting with Sound

Kathy and I created a science center for experimenting with sounds. Here we used simple, well-known activities to create different sounds, such as putting different amounts of colored water into tall glasses and gently tapping the sides of the glass with a wooden mallet. One child discovered how to make a different sound by dragging the mallet along the side of the glasses.

One day as I sat and listened to the sequence of sounds a child was playing on the water glasses, I decided to record her sequence in polka dots with crayons the same color as the water in each glass, so that I could play it back to her. I wrote this down in a linear sequence. She paid little attention to what I was doing until I asked if she could "do that part again because it had been too fast for me to record." Thereafter she began to play slower and would glance to the side at my paper to make sure I had recorded the right colored dot to match the glass. Then I asked if I could have the mallet, and I proceeded to play her sequence of notes, pointing to each colored dot as I did. She was amazed.

The children found the idea of writing down the sequence of "notes" they played on the glasses exciting, and four or possibly more composed their own songs. The literacy aspect of writing down the sounds amazed me. Some played a note, then recorded the corresponding colored dot. Others played a sequence of notes and then did their recording, and I could not be sure they recorded what they actually played in a perfect one-to-one correspondence, but it did not matter. The interesting aspect was that they did read and play their recorded dots in an exact one-to-one correspondence. They especially enjoyed having their teachers and classmates "read" their recordings and play their songs.

In attendance time we used a drum to tap out the syllables in the children's names. One girl was very excited to identify the names with the same number of syllables as her name, which had three.

Creating with Loose Materials

Of course the cut-and-paste area continued to be a hub of activity with children often constructing their own instruments, as described earlier. In addition, one child undertook a project that amazed me. Sarbjot was fascinated by the acoustic guitar. He made several sketches of it and, wanted to make a guitar of his own. He found a box of the right size and rubber bands, which he attached. He also made a carrying case for the guitar. I found it interesting that even though Sarbjot said he

F<small>IGURE</small> 2.2. On the left: Sarbjot's observational drawing of a real guitar appears to show 3 strings. On the right: Rayanna may have drawn 8 strings, or 7, or 6 with the edges of the fret board framing them. What is clear is how difficult it is for a child to coordinate the necessary reference points, such as where the strings begin and end, and how carefully she has tried to "follow" the strings.

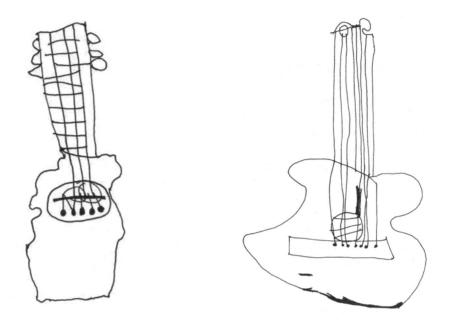

"loved" his guitar, he was willing to share it with his Grade 3 reading buddy. In a photo of a group of children with instruments, Sarbjot is curved around his guitar, holding it carefully. One day he said, "The Music Man I am!"

Anytime Becomes Music Time

The kindergarten rhythm band instruments and the children's own hand-made instruments became a permanent part of our music time at the end of the day. In addition, small groups of children would organize their own bands and proceed to march around the room during regular activity time. A drummer and tambourine player would start a band, while a boy behind them would go about his block building with hollow blocks. Often other children would join the band, or some would simply look up from their own work to see what was going on and then continue. Kathy and I disagreed about these spontaneous bands: I have a high tolerance for noise and it did not bother me, but Kathy found it "too loud," so eventually we would redirect them. Kathy noted, "Although it was difficult some-times to adjust to the noise level, I also felt it was important to allow the children an opportunity to play their music." We thought we should take the instruments outside during outdoor play, but unfortunately we never did. I would have liked to see whether the children eventually lost interest in their spontaneous bands or developed their own noise controls, or whether a band would have left the classroom and taken over the hall. Because we stopped it, there were interesting possibilities in their own actions that we did not discover. And yet, they really did get to play their music.

TEACHER REFLECTIONS

The excitement, interest, and emotional response of the children, and the feeling in the classroom during this exploration of music, is hard to capture and describe, but it is somewhat like electricity. When Carol Anne and I were working on this chapter, she asked me to "open up that statement a little, say how it is like electricity." I thought, "She asks such tough questions." I would say it is like really being "alive." Every part of the classroom has a sense of wonder, of brightness. It's an alertness, a sense of anticipation that something special is going to happen or is happening. It's a feeling that is hard to describe, but I feel it and I know the children do too. Kathy said, "It was so much fun; it was not like work, but rather I had a chance to 'play,' release my inner child, and learn from the students."

My documentation of this work with music consisted mostly of taking photographs and capturing some of the children's dialogue. The bulletin board outside our room was used to share our experience with the school population (parents, children, and other teachers). I enlarged some of the photos, which for me told the story. They captured the children's focus and delight. Because the children's coats were in the hall, they would see and chat about the images as they arrived or got ready to go home each day. My teaching colleagues were particularly amazed by the observational drawings, amazed that they were done by children in kindergarten because of the detail and quality of shapes they had captured. I did not feel I had done a very good job of documenting although we had done what we could, perhaps because what I did do was track which expectations in the written curriculum document (Ministry of Education and Training, 1998a) were "covered," that is, embedded so inherently in the activities that they did not require teacher instruction.

It was unbelievable how many of the kindergarten expectations (Ministry of Education and Training, 1998a) were met in this one project. First of all, the making of personal instruments brought into play science, the arts, language, and mathematics. In science, demonstrating an awareness of characteristics of common materials and making things using a variety of tools and techniques was demonstrated by children who made instruments, both simple ones like the shakers and more difficult ones like guitars. In the arts curriculum, they are expected to "express ideas through a variety of media," "perform in a group," "identify familiar instruments," and I saw this again and again both in their play and in what they made. In math, they are asked to create and copy patterns, and the children who made up songs with the colored water were doing this. When we wrote the songs down, we were engaging in literacy activities. The children understood "that writing conveys an idea or message," as the expectation states. As teachers, we are also supposed to think about "employability skills" and here are a few that this emergent curriculum met. The children were creative problem solvers (this was incredible, like a thread running through our days together). They demonstrated positive attitudes and behaviors, worked well with others, and showed continuous learning. They planned, designed, and carried out under their own steam, making an instrument of their choice or composing a song or creating a band. But for me, the most important part was the children's freedom to play and to be creative, and I mean "play" in a very broad sense.

CAROL ANNE'S COMMENTS

Nancy's story shows how difficult it is to *see* the children's agenda. Because teachers' minds are so full of multiple agendas for what to do, and because pressures to teach literacy and numeracy have increased, it is very difficult for teachers to notice what is outside their agendas. Nancy makes noticing what children are doing and thinking part of her conscious agenda: their natural activity had been sustained for several months when she decided to make it part of the official curriculum by developing music activities. Observing children's interests requires a conscious mental set of flexibility, like leaving a space, or creating an opening in the teacher's agenda, in which something unexpected might appear. Teachers have to override their own agendas in order to take up the children's. Without preparedness to listen and notice what is coming from the children, nothing emergent could possibly happen.

Yet it is more than noticing: it requires the capacity to take that interest and expand it into activities for the entire classroom. It is expansive in that it opens out into more, and inclusive in that it wraps children's interests into the official curriculum. A teacher's willingness to accept and work with what emerges from children as part of her teaching agenda is, in addition, a fundamental lesson to children about being given the right to participate in a democratic lifestyle in responsible ways.

How do teachers create spaces or openings in the crowded time and space of schools in which to notice something interesting emerging from children? Something to watch for in the chapters that follow is how each teacher or principal found her own way to create a time and space in which curriculum might begin to emerge.

CHAPTER 3

To Make a Car
Physics in Motion

Shaune Palmer

"To learn is a satisfying experience," said Malaguzzi (1998, p. 67) in describing how the children of Reggio Emilia schools for early childhood education take an active role in the construction of their learning and understanding. This is also true for adults (Mackeracher, 2004). It was certainly accurate for me. I was in my 4th year as a school principal when I enrolled in a masters program at a university and took a course introducing the Reggio Emilia approach to early childhood education. In Reggio schools "adult and child roles are complementary: They ask questions of one another, they listen and they answer" (Malaguzzi, 1998, p. 69). The curriculum is not predefined but rather a dynamic process of inquiry that develops with common interests shared by the adults and children alike. I was enthralled with the level of thinking and visual representations produced by such young children. How did the Italian educators get this to happen? Could I generate such high levels of engagement and intellectual curiosity for myself and my students in an investigation?

One day a visiting science teacher was in the school working with one of the Grade 2 classes. The visitor had provided the students with a pattern to create a paper and cardboard vehicle. The vehicles did not function well, much to the disappointment of the children. I wondered what thought went into the making of it for the children and whether they knew anything about the design factors that influence the movement of a vehicle. The children were able to follow the instructions, but I found this limiting, and I knew much more could be provided to them using an inquiry process.

Next door in the adjacent classroom I noticed much excitement from the other Grade 2 students who saw the cardboard cars produced by their peers. During dismissal time, I overheard questions and responses being tossed back and forth by the students. This excitement showed me there was interest and motivation from students in the adjacent Grade 2 class. A quote from Jones and Nimmo's (1994) book came to mind: "Children whose own interests are acknowledged and supported don't need to be motivated to learn: their own excitement will keep them learning" (p. 127).

I also was interested in the physics of motion. Science was an ideal curriculum area because it allowed me as a teacher/principal to focus on the integration of curriculum. Language and mathematical development could be enhanced and the medium promoted an activity-based, inquiry-based approach, appropriate for young children. I knew from the Reggio Emilia approach to early childhood education that "adults' and children's minds meet on matters of interest to both of them" (Katz, 1998, p. 36). A good project is when children and teachers are equally engaged in the activities and ideas being investigated. Both of them progress together as researchers, seriously undertaking the work at hand, revising and revisiting knowledge with each new task (Katz, 1998).

The Grade 2 teacher and I together selected six students who expressed interest in joining a small group to investigate movement ideas with me. In making the selection, we considered students who would be open to the ideas of one another, who would mix well together, who had a range of strengths and weaknesses academically and who would benefit from the opportunity to participate in such an endeavor. Two others were on standby if any of those chosen did not seem interested enough to participate in a long-term, in-depth investigation. Six seemed a reasonable number so that the most intense learning and collaboration would be possible. In fact, all six students stayed focused on the project for 6 weeks, meeting about three times a week for an hour and a half each time. The group consisted of four boys and two girls who came from a variety of racial and social backgrounds. One student received support from a specialist teacher.

"Another customary practice in Reggio Emilia is that before the children actually gather to begin the project, the adults involved meet to discuss various possibilities, hypotheses, and potential directions that the project might take" (Rankin, 1998, p. 218). This was true in our case. The Grade 2 teacher and I sat together to imagine areas of investigation the children might propose. But in addition, we reviewed the Grade 2 science curriculum expectations on Movement (part of the Structure and Mechanisms curriculum strand), especially the science section outlining Developing Skills of Inquiry, Design, and Communication (Ministry of Education and Training, 1998c). This section was in keeping with our intent to create a community of inquiry. Some tensions occurred for me in using sections of the curriculum guide as it predefines and "dictates" what the children will do, such as compare the motion of similar objects made with or filled with different materials (e.g., ways in which baseballs and tennis balls bounce; ways in which film canisters containing different materials roll down a slope). In contrast, emergent curriculum emphasizes the children as protagonists, creating their own learning in concert with their teachers. The learning is negotiated by the players (Jones & Nimmo, 1994). However, I was confident that the children would learn a great deal about the topic and meet most of the curriculum expectations through a project that permitted them to interact with a small number of classmates in a focused, in-depth manner. I did gather a number of fiction and nonfiction books, brainstormed possibilities using a web, and looked through curriculum resources to help me explore the range of ideas that might occur as I worked alongside the children. Rinaldi said, "If adults have thought of 1,000 hypotheses, then it is easy to accept the fact that there can be 1,001 or 2,000 hypotheses. The unknown is easier to accept and adults are more open to ideas when they have generated many potentialities themselves" (as cited in Rankin, 1998, p. 218). At this point, the teacher began this unit of study with her class and I began to work separately with the small group.

My framework for the project was adapted from the Reggio dinosaurs project described by Rankin (1998) and included these five aspects:

1. The teacher emphasizes the importance of the group working together as a community.
2. The project starts with a graphic and verbal exploration.
3. The project develops based on the interests of the children.
4. The children require ample time for their investigations.
5. The children and teacher share the project experience with other children and adults in the school.

ENGAGING THE CHILDREN'S INTEREST

All good projects begin with a trigger to initiate motivation (Malaguzzi, 1998). I used the picture book *The Mice and the Clockwork Bus* (Peppe, 1986) to set the stage for generating possible interest. The story is about D. Rat who runs the only transportation service in town using his bus made from a roller skate. The mice that take this bus are concerned for their safety and feel the owner, D. Rat, is only concerned with profits, so decide they will build their own bus, using materials from D. Rat's own junkyard. During the reading of the narrative, I invited the children into the story using drama and role-play techniques to increase their understanding and enjoyment of the conflict between the mice and D. Rat. The children were very interested in the illustrations of how the mice used everyday objects to construct their own bus, and commented:

> They use a lot of different stuff, not stuff for mice.
> They are creative, like scientists.
> They are recycling materials to use them in a different way.
> They are working well together, cooperating—no arguing. I bet that will help them build a good bus to challenge D. Rat.
> Yes, I like the author's ideas of using a clock for the motor.
> Are we going to do this?

Following the reading, we looked at nonfiction books and played with a variety of toy vehicles I had gathered together. Later each student was asked to select and sketch an appealing car (see Figure 3.1). Visual representation is part of the graphic languages of learning so important to the Reggio Emilia approach. It is a very important tool of communication and at times, simpler and clearer than words. When drawing, children are selecting what they think is important. It provides a reflective time to consolidate their thoughts and previous actions. The drawings can also be used later by teacher and students to revisit what happened that day (Malaguzzi, 1998).

FIGURE 3.1. Children's drawings of their toy cars, including the underside.

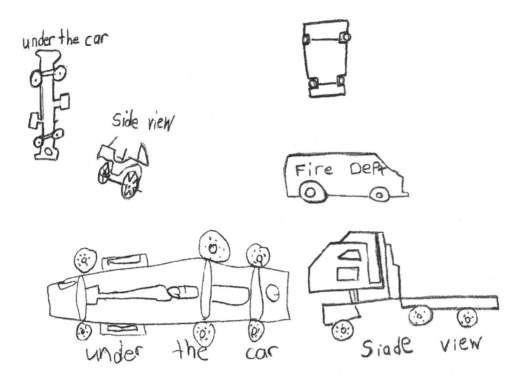

ESTABLISHING A CLIMATE FOR A LONG-TERM PROJECT

These beginning sessions were about rapport building. The children still needed warming up and settling into a new way of working. They had not worked with me very often and we were together establishing a different relationship. The children were familiar with me and were accustomed to my visits when I would sometimes read a story, teach a lesson, talk about recess issues, or help a student, but were quite surprised to learn that I was a teacher. They fired many questions at me as if convincing themselves I had sufficient experience to "handle the job." It was all in good fun, but I sensed that two of the children were skeptical and needed convincing while the rest were excited about the process and felt it was rather special to work on a long-term project with the principal. Talk would be integral in the development and success of the project so I spent time reinforcing the importance of listening to one another, helping each other out, and considering different view points, even ones that at first might seem radical. Thinking, experimenting, and inquiring as scientists intrigued them. I capitalized on this by pointing out to them how they already behave as scientists many times in their own classroom when they observe patterns in numbers, in literature, in their environment, and when they sort objects according to rules or generate questions and try out new ideas to test emerging theories. I tried to use examples from current topics and activities that were ongoing in their classroom. I made a point of visiting their class at other times to make these links for the children when I observed them using the process skills necessary for scientific inquiry. This helped them to develop confidence that they were up for the challenge and also made these skills transparent to them. I wanted to motivate the group so they would see the project as their own (Rankin, 1998). It was also important that each child would be valued by all members—as important as the actual project itself.

IMMERSING THE CHILDREN IN EXPERIMENTATION

We had a conversation. I showed them their previous sketches and comments I had written down when they were with me the day we drew the vehicles. I very much identified with Cadwell (1997) who describes how unsure she felt in the art of conversation with children when she began. The teachers in Reggio Emilia spend much meeting time devoted to developing good questions, to timing the delivery of their questions, to facilitating the conversations, and to ensuring participation of every child (Cadwell, 1997). After some discussion, I asked them, "What makes the cars go?" The group generated many ideas, such as the importance of the wheel shape, the number of wheels, the size of the wheels in relation to the chassis, the requirement that the wheels attach to the vehicle, and the need to push or wind up the car on a flat surface to get it moving or to send it down a ramp using gravity. I laid out materials—straws, wooden skewers, boxes, a hole punch, plasticene, plastic lids of various sizes, beads, large juice caps, and film canisters—to use to experiment with these ideas. The students became interested in the placement of the axle between two wheels. Why was it in the middle of the wheels? What if the axle were placed elsewhere? How would that affect the movement of a vehicle? The children built several sets of wheels with axles in different positions. Here are their comments based on their observations after playing with their constructions:

- We made different axles and they all did different things.
- The axle at the top of the wheels was really bumpy.
- Two axles are very slow.
- The axle in the middle was balanced.
- The best placement is in the middle because it has a smooth movement. It also goes faster. The top is too bumpy.
- If one side of the wheel was too heavy, when I used the plasticene as a nut to hold the wheel in place, it would not go straight, it went curved.

SETTING UP A PROVOCATION

Reggio teachers "help children find problems that are big enough and hard enough to engage their best energies and thinking over time" (Edwards, 1998, p. 187). My interpretation is that Reggio educators would say teachers have misinterpreted children's interests if children lose engagement. Katz and Chard (1998) advise that a distinction be made between providing opportunity for child-initiated spontaneous activity about a topic and investing in a long-term effort focused on it. I knew that I hadn't selected a task as yet that would entice and further challenge learning opportunities. More exploratory activities were required to permit joint problem solving and dialogue that generated possible theories to test. I set up a series of ramps of varying heights and asked the children to select a car to travel the ramps. The children repeatedly sent their car down the ramps, discussing their observations and making adjustments each time to improve the car's performance. They wanted their cars to go straight down the ramps, onto the floor, and travel some distance. Some cars veered left or right. In response, a few children exchanged their cars, noting mechanical deficiencies in their toy cars. The group also widened the ramps and eliminated pushing the car at send-off because the force was either too strong or their hand motion contributed to poor directionality. They selected a thin hard-cover book which could be lifted up as a kind of gate as a solution. Once the gate was discovered, the notion of competition entered into their thinking and a lively discussion ensued about maintaining the same conditions for each vehicle so the competition was fair. It was here that I more actively entered the interaction. The children were getting to the scientific notion of a fair test and I believed that my support would contribute and further shape their thinking to fit the demands of the situation. I also suspected that a good understanding of a fair test would be a concept that would be needed in future investigations.

The next session I asked them to measure the distance their own car traveled on all three ramps of varying heights and to discuss their findings. I chose this because the children were still excited with the cars that traveled far across the floor. When they recorded their observations on paper using a sketch, numbers, and words, they all wrote that the higher the ramp, the faster the car went. At first, I was confused: I thought the children would conclude that there was a relationship between the height of the ramp and distance, as all the children were accurately measuring with the meter sticks I had provided them. Why did they say the car went faster?

Gradually, upon reflection, it became clear to me from my observations and from the conversations I had tape-recorded that the children did understand that the higher the ramp, the farther the car traveled, but *they were more interested in the speed* of the car. In fact, they could see with their eyes how far the car traveled and clearly understood the relationship between height and distance without having to measure. Although initially disappointed, I became excited that perhaps I had discovered a *cognitive knot* for all of us to investigate, a "moment of cognitive disequilibrium, containing possibilities for the regrouping, hypothesis testing, and intellectual comparison of ideas" (Edwards, 1998, p. 187). I understood it as the teacher's job to notice these knots and bring them to the attention of the students.

THE COGNITIVE KNOT

"An emergent curriculum is a continuous revision process, an honest response to what is actually happening. Good teachers plan and let go" (Jones & Nimmo,

Figure 3.2. Shaune's cognitive knot: A child's conclusion is not consistent with the recorded data.

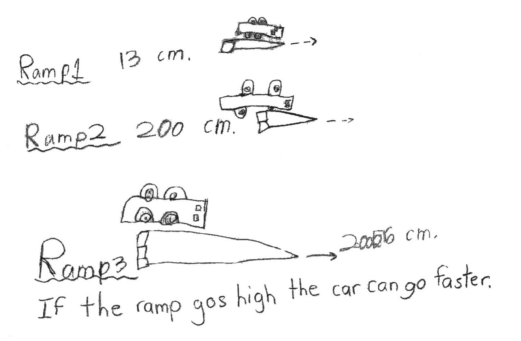

1994, p. 12). I thought I was paying close attention to the children, but perhaps I was being too influenced by my own good intentions. The use of the meter stick to measure distance was my focus. In early childhood education, teachers must remember that they teach children, not curriculum: significant interactions, observations, and challenges arise that can lead us in new directions. As teachers, we need to exercise flexibility so learning opportunities are more responsive and meaningful for students. This is what I needed to do.

I showed the children their work and read back to them their theories presented to me the day we discussed ramp height and distance. This documentation allowed the children to revisit their experience and helped them with "further insights that will motivate further questions and group activity" (Edwards, 1998, p. 183). Below are the theories I read back to them:

- The higher the ramp, the faster the car goes.
- Of course it goes faster, the car has speed. Look at ramp 3. Look at how high it is!
- The car picks up speed on the higher ramps and goes farther as a result.
- We are good scientists because we are good at measuring. On my paper, here, the numbers get bigger. The car goes faster. And the car goes farther.

I asked the students, how do you know the car went faster? Did we measure the speed? What was the purpose of the rulers? Much excited conversation followed where they agreed that they had not measured the speed, but were convinced that their theory was correct. The car goes faster on the higher ramps and as a result, travels further on the floor.

When I asked them, how could we measure the speed to prove our theory that there is a relationship between speed and distance, they gave a variety of suggestions:

- We could clap it.
- No, we would all have to clap at the same time. That would be too hard.
- How about stomping? No, that's the same as clapping.
- We could time it. Do you have a stopwatch, Ms. Palmer?
- You know what? The music teacher has a metronome.
- What's that?
- You know, in the music room, it's electronic. I have one just like it at home. I take piano lessons and I use it to play to the beats. That would be perfect. Can I go get it?

The children designed their own experiment modeled on the ramps set out the previous day. This time they focused on measuring the speed of the cars traveling down the ramp by counting the beats of the metronome, which they set at 160 beats per minute. They decided that every car's speed would be tested three times on the high ramp and three times on the low ramp. This would ensure fair results. They would also be able to tell how far an individual car went by placing a masking tape strip where the car finished landing. This way they could test their theory about the relationship between speed and distance. Great excitement arose when their theory was proven correct (see Figure 3.3). One child commented that this was not Grade 2 work; it must be at least Grade 4 work, and they were all pretty smart. They jumped up and down, congratulating each other for being such good scientists.

EMOTION AND LEARNING

Teachers have long known from experience that emotion and learning are closely connected. When students solve problems, they have feelings of pleasure and satisfaction. More recently, however, neuroscience tells us that the positive emotions in learning are generated in the parts of the brain that are used most heavily when students develop their own ideas (Zull, 2004). This cognitive knot, which was solved through the children's own problem solving and their ensuing excitement, offers anecdotal evidence for this argument. I hypothesize that the Reggio Emilia approach of working with young children to promote their own inquiry may actually produce physical changes in the brain in two ways. First, neuroscientists know repeated practice of an activity or concept causes neurons in the brain to fire frequently, grow, and extend themselves outward toward other neurons, creating greater mastery with each try (Zull, 2004). The notion of spiraling, the continuous cycle of revisiting and rerepresenting used in Reggio schools, may help explain the high level of understanding and visual representations produced by very young children. Reggio children have multiple opportunities to coconstruct and develop knowledge and visual skills with their teachers. The teachers look for future situations where previous learning could be progressively extended or revised by children making sense of new information and experiences. Second, neuronal networks, known metaphorically as "the knowledge highway," also require the chemicals of emotions to keep buzzing. Positive emotions create emotion chemicals that improve the synapse strength and the responsiveness of the neuron networks (Zull, 2004). Because children in Reggio schools construct their own knowledge in part through projects of great interest to them, children feel proud and delighted with their discoveries. My Grade 2 group, testing their own hypotheses, was having a similar experience (see Figure 3.3).

THE DERBY

Curriculum emerges when a teacher is paying attention to the children and is willing to embrace the unexpected (Jones & Nimmo, 1994). One day, several children

FIGURE 3.3. Child's explanation: "My theory is that the higher the ramp, the faster the car goes and the farther it goes. I proved my theory by counting the metronome beats on all three ramps. On the highest ramp, the car had the least [sic] number of beats and went the farthest. On the lowest ramp, the car had the most beats and hardly went anywhere. The middle ramp results were in the middle."

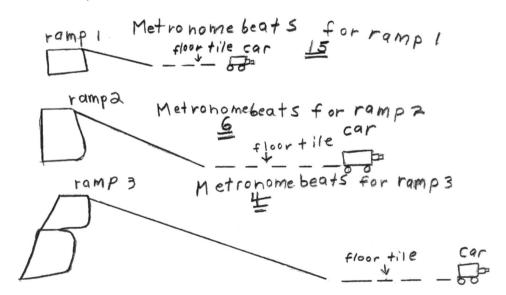

suggested they could build their own individual cars, different from the cars that the other Grade 2 class had made. They wanted to make their own cars and hold a car derby where the cars would be awarded prizes for different attributes. They suggested prizes for the hottest-looking car, the luxury car, the fastest car, the car that goes the furthest, the smoothest ride, and the car that can do the best trick. Here was an idea to embrace. We agreed we could find excellent materials at the new Home Depot store a few blocks away. We walked to the store one afternoon and went up and down each aisle choosing materials such as wooden dowels, wheels, washers, rubber plumbing fittings, Velcro strips, numbers, clothes pins, and fasteners. Quality materials are very important as they produce greater satisfaction for the learner because

> each material offers its own particular qualities to the child and each child offers his or her particular qualities to each material. Each new material gives the child a chance to build another kind of understanding of the richness and complexity of the world. (Cadwell, 1997, p. 27)

The next day, the students selected materials to construct their own vehicle. The task proved to be very challenging. For instance, several students wanted the axles to be placed through the chassis of the vehicle. When they did this, they discovered the axles were on a slant and resulted in the vehicle moving in a circular fashion. It took many attempts before finding a workable solution. Others experienced difficulties with the wheels they had chosen. The wheels were too small for the chassis and made it drag along the floor. Some chose rubber plumbing fittings that were wide and thick but also hollow and had to be filled in with something. Furthermore, each structure had to hold a rotating axle. We were all a little discouraged when confronted with the challenge of working with materials unfamiliar to us. I realized that they needed my help and advice so as not to be defeated by the materials (Edwards, 1998).

We spent several days experimenting with the potential of the materials. Would the objects they had chosen do what each child hoped they would do and would the materials available to them solve the technical problems they were experiencing? I was surprised how this investigation to design cars picked up motivation and enthusiasm with each day. It was truly rewarding to me as a teacher to watch the children tackle each session with further revisions in mind based on new knowledge acquired the previous day. The whole exercise was consistent with the goal of Reggio teachers who do not make learning smooth and easy but stimulate it by making "problems more complex, involving and arousing" (Edwards, 1998, p. 185). I understand that Reggio teachers do not offer solutions but stretch the children toward finding their own answers.

The last afternoon of the project, the group held the car derby and prizes were given all round. Many members of their class and a few teachers came to watch and try out the cars. The children were now a very tightly knit group and there was a great sense of pride and satisfaction in the work they had accomplished.

TEACHER REFLECTIONS

Learning in tandem with the children was truly a rewarding and stimulating experience for me as a principal. It was fun coconstructing the learning process with the group because we were often presented with unexpected challenges. I feel certain that emergent curriculum stimulates high levels of thinking and engagement and offers teachers wonderful insights into themselves and their students. Coconstructing learning with students is possible in all areas of the curriculum and does not have to exist only as part of scientific inquiry in the science curriculum.

Documentation Guides Planning

The documentation process of tape-recording the students' conversation was extremely useful. By recording, then transcribing and examining the conversations at the end of the day, I could retrieve more accurate data about the children. I found there were two kinds of conversations. One kind was the dialogue that occurred while the children were immersed in their action-oriented investigations. These revealed the lively debates, questions, analyses, and revisions that transpired as they interpreted each other's perspectives and made sense of the knowledge they were acquiring. The other kind of conversation was more orderly as it involved the whole group seated together. I used the transcriptions, which were printed on chart paper, as a springboard for discussion and to be the memory for the children (Edwards, 1998). Interestingly, I found that I had to do little preparation for upcoming sessions other than preparing the most recent transcription because the rereading of the previous discussion set them up to clarify or dispute what had been said and assisted them in determining the next steps. In others words, the documentation served to drive their agenda. The process also gave me better insight into what was really said and allowed me to look for patterns that could be developed into challenging investigations.

As a principal, I recognize that teachers have a tendency to see and hear what they want to see and hear or can't focus fully on every word because they are always multitasking in a class of children. Furthermore, an overly dense, predefined curriculum for young children creates pressure for teachers to focus on their agenda for teaching rather than take the time to pay close attention to the script being played out by the children. Although "documentation is not a form of assessment of individual progress, but rather a form of explaining, to the constituents of the school, the depth of the children's learning, and the educational rationale of activities" (Forman & Fyfe, 1998), I would argue it was also an effective assessment instrument in the sense that it highly influenced my teaching and facilitated my decisions. I was better able to gauge when to help and when to step back. I believe my questioning ability also improved as it was based not on recollections but on authentic recorded dialogue, which I reviewed before meeting the children. Other staff members were quite surprised at the level of conversations held by the children and this recording process made the children's thinking visible to them.

Engaged Attention Guides Responsiveness

There were clear benefits of using an emergent approach. For teachers, it is just more interesting and thought provoking. For the children, the approach is more respectful of them as learners since the documentation helps guide teaching decisions. Coconstruction with students requires teachers to develop their observation and listening skills. I must have an engaged attention in order to be responsive to the children. There is a "change from teaching children to studying children, and by studying children, learning with children" (Forman & Fyfe, 1998, p. 240). There was also direct demonstration of the intellectual processes used by young children. Finally, children's interests are acknowledged and developed with other peers who share similar goals. Each member of the intimate group brings different talents and experiences to the project, thereby advancing the learning for everyone. There is a great sense of satisfaction and respect for other learners, including the teacher, because all have created and developed the path of learning together.

Were there any challenges? Not many, if one is able to give up control as the sole owner of knowledge. There were certainly time and reporting constraints. I was very conscious that another unit of study had to be done for report card purposes in spite of the fact that the students could have taken the project further. I made some decisions on what to pursue and what to discard based on my timeline. Additionally, I found that by slowing down and having the children stay focused on what was important for them, learning was better consolidated and will more likely last beyond the specifics of this project.

One of the most enduring understandings left with me after this process is stated well by Malaguzzi (1998): "What we do know is that to be with children is to work one third with certainty and two thirds with uncertainty and the new" (p. 89). It is this challenge of working in the unknown that keeps us interested as teachers.

CAROL ANNE'S COMMENTS

Shaune's project shows how a teacher can take an aspect of standardized curriculum such as a science unit, and an oft-repeated way of doing it (have the children make axles, use ramps, conceptualize a "fair test"), and open it out into more expansive inquiry- and arts-based processes that permit genuine questions, problem solving, and new ideas to emerge. This chapter is helpful in showing how standardized curriculum can be taught in a way that permits children to take ownership of their own ideas and work collaboratively with teacher and other children toward shared goals. Shaune's acceptance of the child's idea of using the metronome to measure speed and of the children's desire to create and race their own cars permitted participation and decision making in an emergent curriculum that took their learning far beyond the curriculum's requirements, yet created positive attachment to the group and motivation for learning. Her project shows how bringing a teacher mental set that allows collaboration, relationship, and "embracing the unexpected" to aspects of standardized curriculum opens learning into excitement for both teacher and children.

CHAPTER 4

The Learner as Protagonist in a Standardized Curriculum
A Grade 3 Unit on the City

Noula Berdoussis, Alice Wong, and Carol Anne Wien

When Noula and Alice were graduate students in a course on Reggio Emilia with Carol Anne, they engaged in a weeklong project in Noula's Grade 3 class. Noula and Alice enacted an inquiry-based emergent curriculum in the face of a standardized curriculum and noticed changes for themselves and the children. The three of us joined together in writing about the project: Noula and Alice worked in the classroom, and Carol Anne was in the background, commenting and discussing.

Ontario has had a standardized curriculum since 1997–98, and provincial testing by the Education Quality Accountability Office occurs each May for 10 days for all children in Grade 3. How does a teacher in a system designed for efficiency, accountability, and high test scores offer nontraditional teaching or learning opportunities that go beyond rote memory, right answers, direct instruction, and testing of young children? This chapter shows one teacher's first attempt.

Noula teaches in the Greater Toronto Area in a culturally diverse K–5 elementary public school with approximately 500 children. The school is surrounded by rental apartments and a new townhouse subdivision. The school tries to reflect the community and meet its needs: There is an on-site government-subsidized day care facility, a snack program for all primary children, on-site annual dental care for students, several special education programs, and an ESL (English as Second Language) classroom. At the time of writing, Noula had 22 children in her classroom, 5 of them with individual education plans for various learning difficulties.

The focus of our study was a social studies unit on urban communities (Ministry of Education and Training, 1998b). In previous years, Noula taught the unit primarily through direct instruction and took the class on a field trip to downtown Toronto, acting mainly as a tour guide who introduces the names and histories of each city structure as they strolled past. Because the standardized curriculum lists expectations item by item, there is a natural tendency for teachers to take expectations up in a linear way (Wien, 2004b): Noula says that in previous years she diligently checked off one expectation after the other, believing that each expectation she covered meant productive teaching. It may have meant teaching, but now she questions if it meant learning.

During the Reggio course, Noula and Alice became increasingly committed to the notion of children as protagonists of their own learning. Noula was about to begin the unit on urban communities—The City of Toronto—and saw it as a perfect opportunity to begin exploring and interpreting for herself aspects of the Reggio Emilia approach that she was learning about with Carol Anne. She invited Alice, a fellow student, to join her, for she believed that through collaboration an enriched experience could emerge for the children and for themselves as teacher-researchers. Noula and Alice were excited, but simultaneously anxious, about what would come of the project. What if the Reggio Emilia approach, developed in northern Italy in schools for children from birth to age 6 (Edwards, Gandini, & Forman, 1998) does not fare well in a Canadian Grade 3 classroom? It is a rather unusual context for emergent curriculum, and the children know little of this way of learning. Noula and Alice's intent was to encourage and extend the protagonist within every child, so that they could be leaders in their own learning. Noula and Alice adapted three aspects of the Reggio approach in particular: the creation of an "amiable" environment for exploration (Malaguzzi, 1998), the generation of a sense of collaborative "we" among the children (Edwards, 1998), and offering the provocation of intriguing questions.

CREATING AN AMIABLE ENVIRONMENT

The quest to interpret the Reggio Emilia approach began with the transformation of an institutional classroom into a more pleasant environment open to all sorts of learning. This was a necessary first step, for we recognized the importance of the environment as a third teacher, a context that offers possibilities to children; an "amiable" environment is a vibrant participant in the children's learning (Malaguzzi, 1998). The conventional public school classroom that we were working with consisted of identical desks and chairs with word and number charts on the walls. A yellow tint suffused the room as a result of the ceiling lights; simply pulling back thick red curtains to let in natural light added warmth. We added plants, cushions, and other aesthetic decor around the room, and rearranged furniture to accommodate a communal supply area and four learning centers. The centers included a sound and paint center, a map center, a construction center, and a light and transparency center. Desks were regrouped, and the once symmetrical organization of the classroom was surrendered. Alice was amused watching Noula's troubled expression as Noula confessed that a round table sitting next to a rectangular desk just didn't look right, but she agreed to try it out.

The purpose of the four centers was to set up contexts in which the children could find their own questions and problems to explore in groups. The paint and sound area, with paint brushes and various sizes of paper, included an audiotaped recording of sounds of the city, which Noula had recorded on a walk downtown. The listener heard people chatting, cars honking, and the wailing of a fire engine as it raced through the streets. The map center included various types of maps, rulers, measuring tape, graph paper, and highlighters. The construction center on two carpets, included wooden building blocks and recyclable materials. The light and transparency center had two overhead projectors, transparent images of Toronto landmarks, lots of paper of various sizes, and pens and pencils. We included the light center because, in Reggio Emilia, light is another "language" of learning and we were curious about exploring it. In the middle of the room was the communal supply center consisting of various types of materials the children could choose freely, for example, cotton balls, colored pens, markers, pencils, rulers, popsicle sticks, wires, paper, plasticine, styrofoam trays, and so forth. The newly organized physical environment set the stage for an enriched learning experience. A new ambience to the classroom was created and gave us a humble sense of accomplishment.

As Noula and Alice prepared for Day 1 of the project, they reminded each other of their objectives in the classroom: "We were no longer the primary source of knowledge nor were we there to discipline and control." As a teacher, Noula was prepared to put aside the structured schedule of the school day, as well as "the exhaustive curriculum that often was the influencing force behind my teaching." Setting these aside inadvertently strengthened her view of children as competent learners, capable of leading adults into an in-depth project involving inquiry, learning, and discovery. With the guiding belief of the learner as a protagonist in mind, "we were more open to listen, observe, and play out our roles as teacher-researchers."

BUILDING A SENSE OF "WE"

As the bell rang, Noula and Alice felt a pinch of nervousness as they anticipated all sorts of "what if's" and wondered how the children would respond. When the children walked in, their eyes darted about and we could sense excitement and curiosity in the air. Quietly the children settled around the edge of the carpet for a brief introduction to the project, and we posed the first questions: What do you know about the city? What do you want to learn about the city? After some discussion, we encouraged the children to select one of their questions and to explore it during the morning: Examples of questions they generated were "Why can't the city be quiet?" and "Where is downtown Toronto?" We invited them to use anything in the classroom that would help their investigation. Following these instructions, the children broke into groups and began exploring the materials and the new environment.

Noula and Alice immediately observed that the children were uncertain what to do, where to begin, and how to proceed. They felt the students wanted information about the expectations and the task at hand, as was the custom in the conventional classroom. As they encouraged the class to explore the materials to find out more about the city, the children repeatedly asked, "What am I supposed to do?" or "Am I allowed to do this?"

The feelings of displacement continued in group work. Instead of children working together, a lack of group effort was obvious as they watched the students work in isolation within a shared space. Within their groups, children rarely spoke with each other. Instead, most project-related questions and confirmation on the validity of a theory or an action would be directed toward Noula. When encouraged to ask their peers, they would either simply let the question go or reluctantly ask another group member. Those who did attempt to seek guidance from their peers were not well received. In fact, they were frequently dismissed or confronted with comments such as "Don't *you* know?"

Noula and Alice continually encouraged the children to communicate with each other. When questions were directed to them, they were careful not to respond with a direct answer but would instead invite children to seek the opinion and help of their peers. With much hesitation, the children began to ask each other. Most of the time, groups were formed after one child began an activity and other children decided to join. As a result, there would rarely be a brainstorming period, a plan, or strategy among themselves on how to proceed in their activity. Disagreements often led to conflict, and group dispersal was the solution.

Because group work was so new to the children, Noula and Alice participated as group members in attempts to mediate group relations until the children felt more comfortable. Even during class discussions, the children were somewhat restless and would whisper to those nearby while their classmate was sharing an idea or responding to a question. Yet toward the end of Day 1, the children began to share discoveries and even the pleasure of group work.

Adding Questions

That evening, Noula and Alice discussed the first day. As the children grew more at ease with the new environment and approach to learning, they felt more confident about continuing to have the children work in collaboration with the materials at the four centers. To extend exploration with the materials and to encourage more hypothesizing and theorizing, they created a question for each center to spark further questions, discussion, and engagement with the materials:

1. Sound and painting center: Painting in response to listening to sounds in the city. Pretend you went on a walk with me, how do you feel?
2. Light and transparency center: Exploring transparent images of city buildings projected on the wall. After working in this center, how do you understand the city of Toronto and its structures?
3. Construction center: Knowing what you know about the city, how can you represent the city of Toronto?
4. Map center: How big or small is Toronto? Where is Toronto in Ontario, Ontario in Canada, and Canada in the world?

Carol Anne sees the questions as providing the children with a broad set of parameters within which to think. Simultaneously, the questions are of a different quality, or type, than usually asked in schools because they invite the children to interpret their world through their own experience and positioning in it. Carol Anne thinks the questions are important in giving the children permission to think in a different way than schools usually offer, and that it was remarkable that Noula and Alice so quickly grasped that a different category of question was required.

Questions as a Provocation

The following day, Noula and Alice introduced the questions for the four centers and the children gathered in their groups. They observed intently to see whether the questions helped children identify and extend areas of interest. What they observed next was very exciting.

At the light and transparency center, Noula found two girls tracing the projected image of Old City Hall onto large paper. The girls quietly concentrated on each pen stroke to ensure precision as they worked to re-create details of the complex structure. Gently, Noula asked what they were doing and they quickly told her that they were working on Old City Hall. "If there is an Old City Hall, do you think there is a new City Hall?" Quickly they said yes and showed her the other transparency. She tried to extend this interest in Toronto's landmarks by turning their attention to the other transparencies and asked, "What structures are these?" She then left them to themselves, secretly hoping that "a seed had been planted." When she later returned to the girls, she found them joined by another interested group, all huddled around books about Toronto. They were excited to share with Noula the name of each structure, its history, and its location, perhaps relevant for the upcoming field trip into the city.

Meanwhile, shared excitement was also being experienced at the map center as four students tried to figure out distances. Alice overheard a child saying that it takes one hour to get from Toronto to the city of Barrie. Alice posed a provocation to question his statement: "If I were to ride my bicycle to Barrie, would it still take only an hour?" Without debate, they all said no. "I was impressed with the ease through which I was able to draw myself into the children's conversation because I was a visitor in their classroom and they only knew me for a couple of days." Turning to the measuring tapes and rulers on the table, one of the students suggested measuring how many inches it was to Barrie. With the knowledge that it took one hour from Toronto to Barrie, he suggested counting the inches to an hour. Mathematical frustration set in and one curious student interrupted and asked, "What are you doing?" The students explained the difficulty they had run into. He asked, "Did you guys use the map scale?" He quickly took charge, taking a strip of paper and making markings on it to indicate the distance that equals five miles. With that strip of paper, which he turned into a portable scale, the group proceeded to measure the distance from Toronto to Barrie. This discovery had a snowball effect as group members started to measure how far the school was from the Eaton Center department store downtown and what possible routes one could take to get there.

Even conflict was passionate. At the construction center, two boys were debating road construction. One child had placed an oversized pylon between two long planks of wood. The two planks were part of a complex highway system. He was immediately questioned by a group member who couldn't understand how the cars would get over the pylon barrier:

"I just don't get it."
"The cars would just go up the side."
"What if the cars are coming from the right and the left and they get
    blocked?"

Noula asked, "Can you use the materials to solve this problem?" and said in our discussion, "I was thinking of the question as the planting of a seed. I left them and later found the road barrier removed and replaced by an intricate bridge."

During this time, a tone of questioning was being established in the classroom. As the children became more comfortable with the constant questioning, they became keen to raise questions, preparing themselves to become active protagonists of their own learning. Carol Anne argues that thinking of questions as "seeds to thinking" rather than queries requiring answers is a major change in a teacher's teaching practice. If the question is a "seed," it is asked for a different purpose than receiving a correct answer; it is asked to stimulate thinking and feeling. To be asked, "What do you think?" is a very different engagement than being asked for an answer.

Settling into Group Learning

By Day 3, the children depended less and less on teacher direction as they broke off into their interest groups. No one asked for help. When Noula or Alice were called over by the children, it was because they wanted to show what they were doing. The children were fully interested, confident, and engaged with the study of the city. When the recess bell rang, it "fell on deaf ears," as the children enthusiastically chose to work through it. Sensing a high level of energy and direction among the children, Noula and Alice stepped back and spent more time and attention on careful listening and observation.

In the midst of the high buzz, one boy sat quietly at a round table examining a book. His attention was focussed on a close-up photo of the CN Tower. Using a gel pen, he carefully drew the tower and shortly after, he started to record interesting facts around his drawing (see Figure 4.1). In a class debate earlier, he had been challenged when he said the CN Tower was the tallest tower in the world. Unable to defend his position, he was now reading, recording, and drawing with great interest. Influenced by his classmate's doubts and the desire to know, he took control over his own learning for he had a stake, a personal investment, in finding the answer.

During Day 3, tragedy struck the city of Toronto. In the planned demolition of an old cinema, a wall collapsed onto a neighboring language school for adults, injuring many inside. One of the Grade 3 children was particularly touched by this event and wrote an article at home about what had happened and how he felt. He asked for a moment during morning gathering time to share it with the class. This event added another dimension to the image of the city: It became more than structures, noise, and traffic, for the children empathized with the people who were injured and felt a part of the community. With this tragedy, the city project had become bigger than the classroom.

CHILDREN AS RESEARCHERS

Noula and Alice planned to provide the children with real life experience by going on a field tip to downtown Toronto, accompanied by parents. Such a trip could

FIGURE 4.1. Information about the CN Tower, carefully recorded as a boy reads about it.

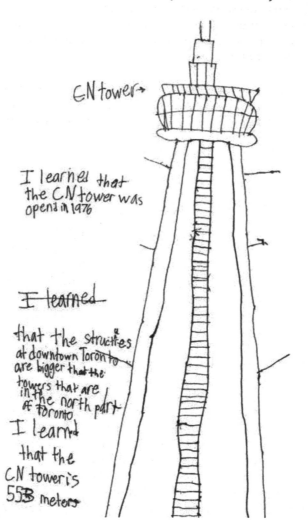

permit connections between children's experience of the city and their classroom study, connections that could become deeper and stronger, provoking them to construct additional layers in their thinking.

Equipped with a camera and an audiotape recorder, they left the school at 9:00 a.m. and boarded the city bus to get to the nearest subway station. Off to downtown Toronto! Each child had a mininotebook with a prompt stapled on front: "During our trip, record what you see, hear, smell, taste, and touch. Record what you learned." On the subway, the children immediately recognized the subway map. They were quick to point out that the map we were using at the map center was outdated because it did not include the newest purple subway line. We started recording their conversations. "There are 13 stops until Queen station"; "I smell gas"; "My ears are popping"; "I just saw the CN Tower!" Noula found herself bothered by one student who shouted out each time the subway doors opened.

Impatiently, I asked him why he was doing this. He said, "I want to hear my echo." His attentiveness to the surrounding environment left me feeling somewhat embarrassed, as I realized how quick we are as teachers to correct children's behavior without taking the time to understand the reasoning behind their actions.

When the class finally arrived on Queen Street, the children and parents followed as Noula and Alice walked toward Old City Hall. They were hoping someone would say something before they passed it. Suddenly, children called out:

"Hey, that's the clock tower of Old City Hall."
"I see gargoyles up there!"
"What's inside?"
"Can we go in?"

Noula and Alice were really excited, realizing that the children were "tossing the ball" (Rinaldi, 1998) and it was up to them to toss it back. So inside they all went, Noula and Alice secretly pleased that the children's desires were shaping the course of the day. As they lined up to pass through the X-ray machine, the security guard was bombarded with questions from a group of fearless children.

"Why do we have to do this?"
"How does it work?"
"Can I put my backpack through the machine?"

They crowded around the screen to examine the contents of their backpacks, pointing and laughing as each bag went through. Alice felt a gentle tug on her sleeve:

Two students wanted to know if they could borrow my tape recorder
to interview another security guard. I gave it to them, and quickly they
went off to conduct their interview. We never found out about the content of the interview until we revisited the tape. Did you know that there
were jail cells in the basement of Toronto's Old City Hall?

As Noula and Alice observed the children's desire to question and explore, they believed the project had become child-initiated as the children took on the role of researchers asking questions.

Leaving Old City Hall with heightened enthusiasm, they then entered the new City Hall. Here the children discovered a three-dimensional model of the city of Toronto. Immediately, this created a buzz of oohs and ahs followed by the repeated comment that the CN Tower *is* the tallest freestanding structure in the world. [We note as this goes to press, that a structure in Dubai has now surpassed the CN Tower.] Even though Thomas had presented his research to the class, the children were not convinced by his findings. Doubts persisted even on the day of the trip, as children who viewed the CN Tower from a different perspective argued that Thomas's research was wrong. Standing before the model was a moment of clarification. For Thomas, these comments provided a sense of validation, for his in-class research proved correct. The children quickly took out their notebooks and recorded their finding.

Observing the children curiously explore City Hall, Noula was excited and spoke into her tape recorder to capture the vibrancy of the scene: "I recorded the things the children said, summarized observations made since their departure, and made a note to myself on my immediate feelings of satisfaction as I watched the children completely involved and respectful of each other and the new space they had entered as guests. The morning passed quickly but we felt that the children were beginning to make connections to the knowledge they themselves had learned in the classroom."

Later that afternoon many children started to wonder why they had not yet seen the Mackenzie House and St. Michael's Cathedral. These landmarks were particularly popular from the light and transparency center for they had been re-created several times by various children in the class. The group that had worked in this center said, "We need to find Bond Street because both structures were located on the same street." Complete jubilation is the only way to describe the children's reaction upon finding Mackenzie House. It was recognized, not by its structural appearance, but by the unique Victorian-style lamppost that stood in front of the doorway, as in the picture of the overhead transparency. Just as adults use structural landmarks to recognize location, so did the children. The children's personal in-class discoveries were coming alive as experience and this was exciting.

The highlight of the day was the glass-enclosed walkway connecting two department stores high above the street. The children looked down and noticed miniature-sized cars and people on the street; they looked up and found a skyscraper towering over them. They tilted their heads, arched their backs, some sat down, and others felt it best to lie down: "Wow, it feels like the building is falling on top of me!" "I feel dizzy!" Something important was happening. Looking straight up at the skyscraper, the children felt small. The skyscraper certainly did not seem so tall from afar. This real-life experience of spatial relations with skyscrapers helped us realize that the children's encounter with distance and perception in drawings, discussions, and reality was an ongoing mystery to them. The children had tossed the ball, and it was time for Noula and Alice to think about how to throw it back in a way that the children would not only want to continue the game, but experiment with many different ways of playing.

"A HUNDRED LANGUAGES"

Malaguzzi's (1998) metaphor that children have a hundred ways of thinking, speaking, and understanding the world acted as a reminder to us. Noula and Alice recalled how a boy wanted to hear his echo and so yelled out every time the subway doors opened; and how the children used a Victorian-style lamppost to recognize the MacKenzie house. These are embodied ways of exploring, understanding, and learning. On the final day, the teachers set the stage for the children to use their "hundred languages" of knowing to share with others their understandings from the trip. They raised the following question for class discussion: "In what different ways did you see the city of Toronto?" At first, the children found the question difficult to understand, but when part of the tape recording from the trip was played back to them, and they heard themselves talking about seeing downtown from up high, down low, and from side to side, their perceptual memories were revisited. The children broke off into their groups and began to find ways to represent the city from varying perspectives.

In the far corner of the room, one group was working with plasticene to represent the city from a bird's eye view. They rolled balls of plasticene, shaping it to make particular downtown structures. What was interesting about their representation of the structures was that every building was in proportion, except for one feature: Why was Nathan Phillips Square was so big in comparison to the other city structures? The group said that they had to make it bigger because it was too difficult to shape the fine details in plasticene. As soon as that was said, they realized that they could experiment with other materials, such as pipe cleaners or popsicle sticks to find one that would allow them to represent the fine details they wished to include. Later, the group reported having difficulty making the CN Tower "stand up." A student suggested making plasticene "Band-Aids" to support the tower from tilting over. The group supported his idea, finding the use of plasticene in this instance to their advantage. What Forman (1996) calls "affordances" of materials (their specific physical properties) affects what children can make with them, and learning these limits is part of understanding mediums of expression. Noula and Alice were impressed by the confidence and ease with which the group switched between materials in order to find the right one to complete their representation of Toronto.

Another group drew from the perspective of being high up on the glass-enclosed bridge. They drew the skyscraper towering high into the sky. Below they drew the street and the cars small on their side. Halfway through their illustrations, this group ran into conflict as they debated where to draw the skyscraper. Visually, it made sense for them to draw the upper part of the skyscraper with no base because that was how they experienced it. However, looking at the whole picture, the bottom half of the skyscraper was missing, as if the skyscraper was built on top of the walkway (see Figure 4.2). Their experience showed the difficulty in representing a complex three-dimensional perspective through two-dimensional drawing. Later, they attempted to draw a three-dimensional skyscraper but it proved too difficult. They left the picture as it was and said, "Next time, we'll use plasticene."

A third group chose to represent the city of Toronto using paint. They cut a piece of large brown paper and planned their mural to include Old City Hall, St. Michael's Cathedral, and the Eaton Centre. First, they used pencils to draw each structure, adding fine accurate detail to each, such as the magnificent stained-glass windows of the Cathedral, the gargoyles of Old City Hall, the multilevel department store with escalators and the pretty water fountain. Then they painted each structure (see Figure 4.3). When the group presented their mural to the class, they explained that it was drawn from the view of a pedestrian "looking at the structures from the sidewalk." In addition, they thanked many of their classmates for helping them finish painting their mural's background in the final minutes before

FIGURE 4.2. Floating Skyscraper: From where the girls were standing inside the glass walkway, the skyscraper above them appeared to have no base.

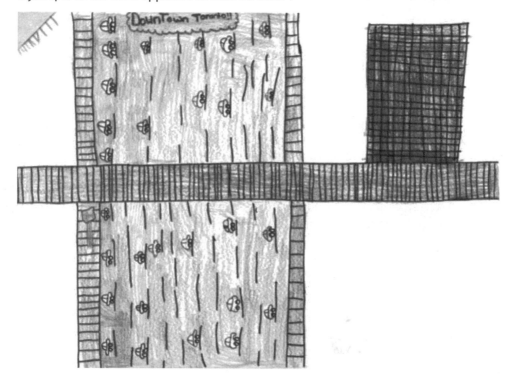

lunch. We were so proud to see the class come together this way. It was hard to believe that this was the same group of children that had been dismissive of each other's ideas and had difficulties coming together as a group. Their shared learning experience had brought them closer together.

Carol Anne thinks the children learned, in part, that their positioning—their perspective—makes a difference in what an individual or group sees. Such an understanding helps students grasp that there is often, but not always, no single right answer, that answers are usually pluralistic, rooted in particular perspectives—cultural, political, perceptual, and so forth. This big understanding about perspective is an important one for contemporary adult life and for values of tolerance, and is an understanding difficult to develop in standardized systems that treat learning as fixed, and outcomes as predictable.

TEACHER REFLECTIONS

Unhurried Time and the Standardized Curriculum

Noula said, "As a teacher, I grapple with time schedules daily as I try to cover curriculum in a preset schedule. I think that school creates an ever-present pressure

FIGURE 4.3. Sidewalk Perspective: The children include details such as St. Michael's Cathedral, gargoyles on Old City Hall, and the escalator in the Eaton Center.

that doing more, and doing it quickly, is better. Such a use of time sets a tone of intensity and influences teaching practices. I think the way I conducted the field trip last year, as a tour guide of sights, is a good example of this intense pressure." The linear lists of expectations that teachers check off give trivial expectations the same space and time as profound ones and coerce teachers toward taking up curriculum in a linear, fragmented way (Wien, 2004b). After this experience Noula and Alice felt that they were beginning to understand the importance of giving children the time to experience, explore, and discover: "The project gave us an appreciation in slowing down and doing less to accomplish more."

Noula found that ironically this year, in less time and with more fun for both the teacher and the students, the necessary social studies curriculum was successfully covered. "When I examined the curriculum requirements after the city project, there was no doubt" that the children were able to:

- Demonstrate an understanding of the characteristics of urban communities (e.g., with respect to land use, transportation, physical features, population, buildings and so forth)
- Ask questions and explore a variety of means to obtain information
- Locate key information about urban communities from primary sources (e.g., field work) and secondary sources (e.g., books and maps) (Ministry of Education and Training, 1998b, p. 32)

The work the children produced during the week was displayed on the classroom walls. It showed directly how the children's thinking shifted over the week toward more conscious awareness about space, size, depth, and distance, and offered many examples of this development. Because our project was to explore an emergent curriculum, we did not document precisely how the expectations were met in nonlinear, nontest ways. The examples in this article, however, offer anecdotal evidence.

An Interpretation of Reggio Ideas

Noula and Alice began with several ideas from Reggio as a focus: creating an amiable environment, supporting collaboration, and using questions as provocations. Carol Anne suggests that enlivening the environment acted as a warm-up for them, settling their own collaboration together, and contributing to the heightened richness of approach they were able to bring to the children during the project. With hindsight, they realized that, "as we agreed to lay out carpets to soften the room or disputed putting a round table next to a rectangular desk, we were benefiting from each other's input, ideas, and experiences. Our shared understanding and attempt to adapt the teaching practices and values of Reggio Emilia created a rich learning environment for our own collaboration."

The values of collaborative group learning had been important to Noula and Alice. Their own collaboration set the tone for the class. For the children, this project was fun. They enjoyed the freedom to wander about in the classroom; they were not only permitted but encouraged to talk in class; and they had more say in what they wanted to learn about and how they were going to acquire the knowledge. Underneath the newfound freedom, Noula and Alice saw some children feeling the appreciation of being listened to. Others realized that their listening skills toward their peers were improving. The value and benefits of working together in groups increased immeasurably over the week. As they watched the children grasp the value of their peers and the benefits of working together, they saw the children developing an awareness of each other's strengths. Children started to understand that they were "resources" to each other's learning (Nimmo, 1998, p. 302).

After the project, the three of us recognized how important it was that Noula and Alice added more structure after the first day. They recognized that they required something to focus children's attention more powerfully and developed the four questions, one for each learning center. Gradually, a style of using questions to stimulate thinking became part of their approach with the children as they supported children in inquiries during their activities.

CAROL ANNE'S COMMENTS

The climate of testing in the spring in Ontario's Grade 3 classrooms is stressful for children and teachers. To offer even a week of investigation focused on unfettered learning, rather than learning leashed to tests, restores wonder, hope, and possibly joy in learning. Such a week promotes mental health in both children and teachers, reducing the potentially harmful effects of environments focused irretrievably on producing high test scores. A rhythm of relaxed learning and a burst of positive energy refresh both teachers and children.

Carol Anne notes Noula's courage as a teacher in attempting an emergent curriculum process in an elementary school setting, especially a Grade 3 classroom, where inquiry and emergent processes have in recent years shrunk from the pressures of standardized curriculum. Noula shows that such emergent approaches work, even for brief time spans such as one week. Carol Anne was impressed that Noula had the energy for emergent curriculum at a time of year when pressure to prepare students for the Grade 3 testing is intense. Paradoxically, Noula is recognized in her school as a teacher who gets strong results on these tests. An approach that sustains inquiry may not be the counterpoint to traditional teaching it seems, but possibly an essential contribution to children doing well.

Noula said, "Something used to be missing from my teaching." From this project, she truly recognized that expectations do not stand in isolation. Although they are treated and written in linear isolation, they are part of the larger whole: children in all the facets of their identities, their cultural backgrounds, and the life of the city as it intersects with them. It is within the context of the whole that personal meaning and learning emerges, something that cannot fit neatly into strict time schedules and learning expectations.

In summary, during this weeklong exploration of emergent curriculum within a standardized curriculum, Noula and Alice explored creating a more amiable environment for children's learning, generating a sense of "we" within the classroom community, and offering the provocation of intriguing questions as seeds to thinking. Inspired by the work of Reggio educators, they created their own first interpretation, one-week long, and through the shared vision among teacher, volunteer collaborator, and professor found a journey into the city that led children onto the path of being protagonists of their own learning.

CHAPTER 5

Wire Bicycles
A Journey with *Galimoto*

Vanessa Barnett and Deborah Halls

To create is to construct, and to construct cooperatively is to lay the foundations of a peaceful community. —Sylvia Ashton-Warner

During an encounter with "The Hundred Languages of Children" exhibit in Toronto, we were drawn to a careful study of the panel *The Intimacy of Wire*. A. Gambetti says of this panel:

> [Its purpose] is to create a kind of open door to the complexity of what [the viewer] will find in the exhibit. Materials—for example, many different kinds of wire—this is something that we have for the very youngest children. We do this so that children will have many different possibilities to explore the world. (cited in Cadwell, 2003, p. 76)

We noticed the strong parallels between the children's investigations with wire and their early gestural drawings. The provocation of experiencing wire as a language with Deborah's kindergarten class was very compelling to us as we observed the playfulness, pleasure, pride, and level of comfort the Reggio children displayed with this material. We wondered how Deborah's class, which has not had exposure to wire, would respond and what they might learn from this exposure. Deborah's lens is as an early-years educator while Vanessa's is that of an artist educator in a major school system. She was able to join the class on five occasions.

This kindergarten class was a combined junior and senior class (children 4–6 years of age). The children were culturally and religiously diverse, and 90% were ESL learners, speaking predominantly Punjabi and Urdu as their first language. Vanessa noted with surprise how quiet many of the children were. The quietness in the classroom was very different from the boisterous interaction that she associated with other kindergarten classes. Many children were still in the "silent period" or preproduction phase of their language formation, and some were nearly silent in class. Our Ministry of Education resource guide (2001) states,

Initially some kindergarten children who are learning English as a second language may go through a "silent period," during which they prefer to observe things around them without comment. They may choose not to talk until they can make sense of the new language through careful listening to the teacher and to peers in the classroom and on the playground or they may talk to others in their first language, unaware that the listener does not understand them. (p. 24)

On Vanessa's first visit, however, Eric shared his excitement about his beautiful shiny black bicycle, a gift for his birthday the day before. Other children talked about their tricycles, while some discussed how they try to ride their two-wheelers without training wheels. Experiences such as wobbling handle bars, falling, not being able to stop, and feelings such as being scared while practicing were disclosed. They loved describing their bikes and made comments like "My wheels are really dirty" or "I have a Dora sticker on my bike."

We realized that here, quite spontaneously, was a wonderful provocation for beginning to explore the linear potential of wire. The possibility of using bicycles for complex investigations of line, shape, and structure, like the wirework we had seen in the exhibit, excited us. Vanessa, originally from South Africa, remembered the children's book *Galimoto* by K. L. Williams, (1990) about a young boy in Malawi, Africa, who searches for scraps of wire to make his own *galimoto* (toy car). William's fascination with the independence and ingenuity of the village children inspired this true story.

We recalled how beautifully the wire installation *The City in the Rain* in "The Hundred Languages of Children" exhibit revealed how the Reggio children make connections among materials and their own experiences. They represented ideas with the wire in the same manner as they would create a carefully observed line drawing. We wondered if the Reggio teachers demonstrated wire techniques to the children. We speculated that experiences with wire strengthen young children's confidence in their own abilities and that the children had developed a comfort level with the wire and could tell stories using the material. Might we begin the process through carefully observed drawings that could be transformed into wire? Should we have a wire installation?

EXPLORATIONS WITH WIRE

The children listened intently to the story *Galimoto* and Vanessa showed them Malawi on the globe. Vanessa brought a collection of wire vehicles that young rural African children made as toys. She remembered young children pushing or propelling their beautifully crafted cars, buses, and airplanes along the sandy potholed roads and ditches by means of a wooden stick, attached to the steering mechanism so they could manipulate their vehicle. The kindergarten children examined the wire motorbike, bicycle, car, and sewing machine she had brought to class and placed them on the overhead projector so their wire images were cast large on the wall, saying things like:

Look at the shadows. It's like our bike wheel in the corner.
I like the spirals on the motorbike engine.
I see thick lines and wavy lines and curvy lines.
They have used different colored wires.

We had an assortment of wire in class in different gauges in clear containers on the workbench. The children began their own investigations, experimenting with the wire cutters to make different lengths. They used different gauges of wire, discussing how best to join them. Thin copper wire was twisted over chrome and bronze shapes. Whimsical circles and spirals suggested creatures and changing ideas:

This is a fish—he lives in the ocean. You can hold it and play with it.
I've made a spiral with little chimes.

Simrat has long braids and spent time making a self-portrait. She wound the wire to create her braids and said, "I can attach them with the thin wire so they will stay."

Many of the wire creations mirrored forms that the children created in two-dimensional artwork. Here were mandala-shaped structures with radial attenuations, and organic and geometric shapes alongside linear interweaving that resembled wire scribbles. We hung these delicate pieces from a branch attached to the ceiling. This was our Alexander Calder–inspired mobile, gently rotating on its axis. The children watched their structures in motion above them in the air, a different perspective from which to see their work.

Bright red pipe cleaners were available as a stimulus to invite the children to make their own small *galimoto*. They began twisting, curling, bending, and joining the different parts of bicycles together talking animatedly about spokes, seats, crossbars, pedals, brakes, and handlebars. We took and later displayed photographs of the children engaged in the wirework and the pipe-cleaner bicycles and were interested to see the children spontaneously looking at the photos in groups and discussing the process. Katz (1998) quotes Loris Malaguzzi on children's experience studying documentation: "Through documentation the children become even more curious, interested, and confident as they contemplate the meaning of what they have achieved" (p. 70).

Observational Drawings of Bicycles

After the first project day, the children had many opportunities to draw and think about bicycles, to visit a corner where a bicycle wheel hung suspended and projected on the wall, and to continue with wire activities available in the room. We were fascinated to observe the changes in the children's drawings over 3 weeks. The documentation that follows shows examples of change. The first drawing of the bicycle was with no previous experience of drawing it, while the second was after many experiences and careful observational drawings of the real bicycle brought into class (see Figures 5.1 and 5.2).

FIGURE 5.1. Gurpreet's interpretation of bicycles before and after close investigation of bicycles.

FIGURE 5.2. Ranveer's interpretation of bicycles before and after close investigation of bicycles.

Gurpreet said of his drawing, "It has a saddle and sloping handlebars." Ranveer said of his first drawing, "I need a bike with training wheels. These wheels are rolling round on the road. It's raining." These examples clearly show the children's increased perceptual awareness and capacity to connect multiple reference points in their thinking represented on paper.

Projecting the Bicycle Image

In Forman and Gandini's documentary of *An Amusement Park for Birds* (1994) there is a sequence where Andrea and Simone create their hypothesis for how a fountain works. The boys are drawing their theory on top of a projected image of the fountain in the park. The projected image gives the boys reference points for their initial drawing, as they think about the fountain and, as Malaguzzi (1996) suggests, "develop theories on how fountains work" (p. 135). We were interested in giving our children a tangible outline as a set of reference points and made two overheads of a photograph of a yellow bicycle that we projected life-size onto large sheets of acetate against a white background. The children were intrigued with the idea of the projected image. They had had prior experience in a previous project of working with projected images of structures they created: They struggled to draw the structures they had built and became frustrated. By projecting the image of a photograph of the yellow bicycle, we allowed the children to revisit this experience and work together in a collaborative way.

Before they began to draw on the acetate there was discussion about the projected image:

> Some lines are thick, some parts are dark, the spokes are very thin.
> There is writing on the bike and it is colorful.
> The wheels are very strong and they look "bumpy."
> That is to make the bike not wobble and slip in the mud.

The children worked in pairs to trace the bike. There was a natural flow—one child finished a section and another was there to step in and draw. It was interesting how often the children drew the shadow and not the outline of the bike. The drawing became organic—their own interpretation—the bike but a guide to the drawing. We switched off the overhead from time to time so the children could observe the drawings and we regretted that we didn't have a real bike as a direct reference. But that was corrected the next day when Deborah brought one in so the children could work directly from it to enrich the drawings through careful observation. We invited the children to focus on specific details like the chain, pedals, and reflectors.

It was exciting to see the focus of the children. They loved the structure of the projected image as a starting point, but once the projector was turned off, the real drawing began. They made directional lines as equivalents for the spokes and darker areas for the surrounding part of the two-toned saddle. Most delightful were the details in the wheels with the rubber tire and traction "bubbles."

Large-Scale Drawings

The children created a large bicycle drawing using the overhead projection and the real bicycle as a frame of reference for their drawing (see Figure 5.3). Deborah noted that she was more relaxed, seeing how confidently the children responded. There seemed to be a transition time in the beginning of the drawing process in which the children tried to organize and become comfortable in their gestural lines. Sometimes they couldn't see the line: "Move your shadow out of my way," was a comment that caused us to laugh out loud.

A group of three began their own drawing, struggling to find space. They came together quickly, discussing, planning, and observing the real bike. Some followed along the shadow outline with their fingers, tentatively, and others drew with such purpose and confidence. Vanessa found it interesting that one child moved to the projector to look at the photograph as a reference for his drawing, rather than looking at the projected image. Others referred to the real bike as they paused in their drawing, looking over often. Two children actually took a walk around it several

FIGURE 5.3. Large scale drawings change how we look, and how we see reference points. It helps us "think big."

times, discussing the kickstand. They added detail not seen in the projection. One child printed his name on the bike and another followed. Deborah said: "I am in awe over their representation of a bike. I must continue to learn to trust and give children the space they need."

Vanessa noticed how the children responded to the project individually, their strengths and interests seeming to dictate their involvement. Some demonstrated organizational ability with the technology of the overhead projector, while others chose to interpret the bike in paint or used wire to make small versions of the bicycle. Some enjoyed using tools to take an old bike apart, while others enjoyed riding bicycles and telling stories about their experiences. Observing their varied responses strengthened our awareness of the necessity of providing many entry points for the children. Varied materials and activities help children express themselves and feel included. Malaguzzi (1998) says of teachers:

> They must know that activities should be as numerous as the keys of a piano, and that all call forth infinite acts of intelligence when children are offered a wide variety of options to choose from. (p. 73)

The children in the class went through an imaginative metamorphosis in their creative process. They began to add to the large projected drawings pinned up on the wall when they had the real bike in the class to observe more closely. Details such as the kickstand and brake wires were added over the original drawing with a black marker. The children added writing too, a combination of letters copied from the lettering on the real bike and their own initials or names. They were curious about how the wheels turn, the texture on the tires, why the wheels are bumpy, the connection of the pedals and chain. They counted the spokes and looked at the pattern they made. In small groups the children came back to the bike to discuss their ideas and hypotheses.

THE BICYCLE SCULPTURE

Working with the real bicycle was a provocation to us to experiment further. From creating small individual pieces with wire, we decided to experiment with the creation of a large collaborative wire bicycle. This was a dramatic shift in scale and medium. We were able to find two large sheets of fine silver and copper mesh from our school system materials resource center, and the children experimented with weaving wire threads through the mesh. We brought in a box of "beautiful stuff" that included screws, bolts, washers, nails, metallic pieces, springs, silver bells, and "found objects" from the resource center. Vanessa recognized, as an artist, that an optimal experience for the collective project required a sensibility in terms of the choices of textures and colors available, and she provided a controlled color palette for the metal shapes and textures. We were interested to see how the children would integrate these textures and materials into the collective wire bicycle. The children spent time getting to know the collection—sorting, classifying, and suggesting pieces as visual equivalents for parts of the bicycle.

Deborah told Vanessa how the children were developing familiarity with words, phrases, and new ideas, but some were still hesitant about saying what they were thinking out loud. In our brainstorming and discussion session it was evident that the children were receptive to new vocabulary and observed their classmates' interactions enthusiastically. They enjoyed participating in all aspects of the classroom activity centers and were drawn to the wire project as it developed. The kinesthetic experience of working with wire gave these children confidence in expressing ideas and feelings and extended their vocabulary. The children's conversation and dialogue reflects the learning that is occurring. In our York University course on the Reggio Emilia approach, Carol Anne spoke of the teacher's role:

> Our task here is to help the children communicate with the world with all their potential, strength, and language, and at the same time overcome any obstacle presented by a culture that tends to impoverish them by undervaluing their capacity for creativity and self expression. (Class discussion, 2007)

Having opportunities to become involved in varied group activities, the children were free to express themselves in ways that were meaningful to them. The power of projects of this kind is that all children can find their own entry points and be drawn into a "long laboratory session where hands work with ideas and inventions to give real dimensions to what will eventually be constructed" (Malaguzzi, 1998, p. 130).

Drawing as a Reference Point for Sculpture

The children placed one of the acetate drawings of the bicycle on the floor and experimented confidently with placement of the wire mesh and found materials. They were constructing knowledge collaboratively as they began to formulate ideas about how to use the wire to form an armature for the bicycle:

> I think we should start with the wheels because they are the biggest.
> We can cut the spoke wires.
> But how will we join them? They will be too short if we cut them.
> Maybe we can have one long wire and wind it around the middle.
> But that will look messy—look at the wheel on the real bike, it is smooth.

Using a roll of thick soft wire mesh two boys formed the outline of the wheels using the drawing as a guide. The ends of each circle were joined with silver duct tape. This metal tape is easy for young children to use.

Gurpreet thought carefully as he created the spokes, considering how they would radiate. He started at a point on the edge of the circle and then brought the wire to the center. He wound the wire over the center point and then took the wire out to another point on the outside of the wheel, securing the wire by winding it around the wheel rim a number of times before cutting it. He gained momentum in creating spokes and was able to repeat the process so that the wheel has many spokes like the bicycle drawing. The frame of reference was important. He stood back and surveyed his work but was unhappy with the center and complained to Murtaaz, "It is messy, it needs a cover like the real bike. I want to make the spokes have a cover like on the bike here."

Exquisite Problem Solving

They riffled through the box of metallic shapes and pulled out a silver metal lid. Murtaaz said, "This will work, I think, but I will need to make a hole in it to make it stay." Gurpreet was wearing a shirt with buttons, and his eyes lighted on the shirt.

> "Look at the button on my shirt, it has two holes, no four holes, and the thread goes through the button and holds the button on my shirt. I can do this with wire!"

> "I know, I know," said Murtaaz. "We can make holes at the workbench with a hammer and nails."

They went to the workbench with two lids, put on hard hats, and searched for the right nail to make the holes. They hammered and measured to see if the wire would be able to thread through the holes, and made two holes in each lid. They thread the spoke covers onto the bike with thin golden wire that they chose, highly satisfied with their work. Rinaldi (1998) emphasizes the importance of listening and paying close attention to what children are thinking and saying:

> Listening means giving value to others, being open to them and what they have to say. Listening legitimizes the other person's point of view, thereby enriching both listener and speaker. What teachers are asked to do is to create such contexts where listening can take place. Listening is thus a general metaphor for all the processes of observation and documentation. Observation involves much more than simply perceiving reality, but also constructing, interpreting and revisiting it. (p. 120)

We realized that we needed to listen for and document these small moments of exquisite problem solving, such as Gurpreet and Murtaaz's jointly constructed connection between buttonholes and spoke covers.

Others came over to see the wheels but pointed out that you can't have wheels with no tires. Ranveer suggested we should use the wire mesh because "it has texture like the rubber tires." This mesh needs adult hands to cut it into long strips that can then be folded for the tires and wrapped around the wheels. The children held the wire mesh as it was cut with wire cutters and then jumped on the folded wire with their shoes to flatten it. The children were also keen to see the shape of the bike emerging with the wheels and overlay the thicker flattened wire on top of the drawing to make the outline for the frame, as well as the saddle and handlebars. Our next challenge was to get the pieces to connect.

As teacher-researchers we were as engaged as the children. After the children left that morning we sat and talked because we felt so deeply invested in the work. This reflective time was enriching because there was focused discussion and much problem solving on everybody's part. We realized that for large projects like this, scaffolding needed to be provided by adults. Work that pushes boundaries by extending knowledge and understanding and making connections doesn't happen in isolation. These discussions reinforced the importance of the relationality that is at the core of Reggio practice. Reciprocal relationships are fundamental to everyone's development, not simply children's. We don't know exactly what we have in mind, but ideas build. As Carol Anne says, "This is like Bruner's [1996] definition of intersubjectivity—'mutually figuring out what others have in mind.'"

Constructing with Wire

The children looked with fresh eyes at the progress they had made on the bicycle thus far, and reflected on the process they had been through. In Reggio the importance of seeing work as a spiral of knowing (Bruner, 1960) is vital to the dialogue—to revisit, discuss, document, and question. Rinaldi (1998) believes that

> the construction of knowledge is a subjective process that proceeds in a spiraling rather than linear or stage-like way; it is clear that our progettazione must involve multiple actions, voices, times, and places. (p. 119)

FIGURE 5.4. Wire bicycle sculpture: The children reflect on their collaborative participation.

We had a new provocation: Will the thin wire that is the outline of the drawing be strong enough to hold the saddle, wheels, pedals and handlebars? Much debate occurred:

This is a bike, but not a really real bike.
We need strong crossbars because if you sit on this bike it will melt.
We need something like a metal bar, but not a metal bar.

The children perceptively recognized that the wire outline of the bike must be joined to the wheels, crossbars, and handlebars. We had thin sheets of aluminum, which were easy to cut and bend. This metal could be wrapped around the wire structure. The children measured the length of the supporting wire bar with string to know how long the lengths needed to be. We cut the sheets and clad the wire outline using a hole punch and golden split pins to close the foil sheets and keep them in place. Now it was time to attach the wheels and handlebars to the frame with thin wire.

The children each decided on which section of the bike they wanted to complete: the saddle, wheels, or handlebars. Finally, wire was wrapped around pencils to make spirals, bells were attached to the wheels to add a joyful tinkling element to the bike, and a discarded metal slinky was reclaimed and excitedly tied to the frame. The wire weaving the children completed during the exploratory work was perfect to go over the saddle and then Harshvir remembered the treasure box and four chrome handles became the brakes and reflectors. The children gathered around and admired their sculpture (see Figure 5.4). Nothing without joy!

The children's investigation raised new questions as we reflected on the way their exploration with wire became a catalyst for further discovery in a continuum of knowing.

TEACHER REFLECTIONS

It has been enormously enriching for us to remember and recount the progression of our journey with *Galimoto*. We have had many insights and have begun to situate them as part of the process through our early experimentation with video, photos, and written documentation. Dahlberg and Moss (2006) describe the work of Reggio as characterized by willingness to "border cross driven by an endless curiosity and a desire to open up to new perspectives" (p. 4). Our journey has embodied a border crossing in terms of putting some of the theoretical ideas of Reggio into practice. We explored how to ask questions of the children to open up dialogue for more questions. We engaged with the language of wire, developing a preliminary visual vocabulary that allowed the children to use thin wire lines to draw forms in space, to understand the potential for joining wire together, and to make forms three-dimensional by layering wire textures onto the linear armature of a wire bicycle.

Tracing the shadows of the real yellow bicycle projected onto acetate with fine black markers was a joyously liberating experience in that it gave the children the confidence to draw on a large vertical format. The children drew the structure of the same bicycle they enjoyed riding, and when the projector was turned off, they took ownership of the drawing by adding lines, shading, and details based on their own careful looking and knowledge of this familiar bicycle. The projected photograph of the bicycle connected the children's kinesthetic riding of bicycles to their early drawings, *galimoto* constructions, large acetate drawings, and the collaborative wire sculpture.

We were pleased that we included the whole classroom community. We wanted all the children to have this experience with wire, especially after the enthusiastic response the initial discussion evoked. What we observed was a balletic choreography where the children moved in and out of the spotlight of the activity. There were core experiences that every child participated in, like experimentating with wire to create the Alexander Calder–inspired mobile, drawing bicycles, and drawing part of the large projected bicycle, as well as working with tissue paper collages. Then there were children who took the lead in the wire bicycle sculpture while others were responsible for the more decorative aspects, adding details and texture to the frame. We were happy with the opportunities for both leadership and participation that the project offered the children. We were also happy with the opportunities for the adults: By collaborating as researchers, we developed a deeper understanding of our own intersubjectivity and became, in the words of Edwards (1998), "dispensers of occasions" (p. 181).

The journey with *Galimoto* was central to the investigation of the class for over a month, with the children reading and writing about bicycles, singing songs about bicycles, drawing, painting, and creating collages about bicycles. Simultaneously, they were riding them outside, in the spring weather. This shared understanding across many modes of experience resulted in increased engagement as well as cooperative learning.

Through the process of our journey we have learned the importance of letting children be masters of their own timing and being respectful of their individual and group learning styles. We have seen that allowing children sufficient time to explore and construct helps them acquire a clear understanding of the problem and reinforces their ability to experiment successfully. In the words of Malaguzzi (1998):

> One has to respect the time of maturation, of development, of the tools of doing and understanding, of the full, slow, extravagant, lucid, and ever changing emergence of children's capacities; it is a measure of cultural and biological wisdom. (p. 80)

To our great joy, on the last day of the project, one tiny child who had scarcely spoken all year volunteered that she had "a pink Barbie bicycle." The bicycle work provided a sufficiently strong link between school and home, different languages and cultures, that she could bring herself into the classroom as a speaker of English and be a full participant.

CAROL ANNE'S COMMENTS

For me, this chapter is an enriching example of how the participation of artists in classrooms changes pedagogy. I do not refer to mere enhancement of curriculum through the arts. Rather, when artists are integrated into classroom processes to work with children and teachers and thus bring their expertise with materials, with design and creating, and their particular aesthetic sensibilities, *pedagogy is transformed* (Wien & Callaghan, 2007): all participants find more in themselves and others than they knew existed. They find the "little room" (Beattie, quoted in Wien & Callaghan, 2007) inside themselves where good ideas and positive feelings might grow. This extended pedagogy occurs here through the combination of using the real (bringing in a real bicycle to ground the project), exploring new material (wire), enlarging the scale of drawing (large projected images), and then combining enlargement of scale with three-dimensional work (the bicycle sculpture). There is no question the children know bicycles—how they are constructed and function—in much richer and more thoughtful ways. There is no question their participation was a delightful engagement that furthered their sense of inclusion in school culture and drew out their participation as second-language English speakers. Fundamental to such expanded possibilities is a teacher who risks uncertainty, who trusts in the development of the children and herself, and who participates equally in the meaningful learning at the heart of artistic intellectual work. To me, this was a beautiful collaboration because of what both artist and teacher brought to the children and because of the synergistic creativity made possible by it.

PART II

LONG-TERM EFFORTS
IN EMERGENT CURRICULUM

CHAPTER 6

"How Big Is Tiny?"
Do Grade 1 Girls Grasp Measurement?

Susan Hislop and Jennifer Armstrong

Why, after all our work to teach measurement in the fall, did the children revert to counting plants instead of measuring the garden area in a spring project? Our biggest challenge continues to be the thoughtful inclusion of math and literacy into the fabric of project work to make learning in these areas more meaningful and authentic. Four years ago our pre-K–Grade 6 urban, elementary school began to investigate the learning experiences of the early childhood schools of Reggio Emilia, Italy, and worked to interpret these learning opportunities in the context of our own setting. Jennifer, as principal, and the teachers were intrigued by the images of the child protagonist represented in documentation and publications from these unique schools (Edwards et al., 1998; Giudici, Rinaldi, & Krechevsky, 2001; Malaguzzi, 1996). We were already involved in an investigation into inquiry and curriculum integration. We wondered about the relationship between our studies and the experiences of the schools of Reggio Emilia. We were also perplexed by the relationship between the provincially mandated curriculum (Ministry of Education and Training, 1997–1998) and the constructivist philosophies we believed to be at the core of our purpose (e.g., Duckworth, 1996; Van de Walle, 2001). Teachers knew they wanted to facilitate understanding as opposed to merely teaching the children, and wondered: Could the children learn more effectively for themselves?

Our teachers had been working with Jennifer, who collaborates with them regarding overall curriculum, on how to incorporate a more problem-based approach to mathematical principles; we meet in large and small groups on a regular basis. Much of what is discussed in these meetings involves children's work, related theoretical frameworks, and our own understanding. The pre-K–Grade 2 team frequently discusses projects and documentation in relation to our interpretation of Reggio processes and principles. Susan teaches Grade 1, and Anna Papageorgiou joins her part-time, documenting class discussions for Susan and monitoring the class while Susan works with a small group. This Grade 1 class was culturally diverse, with children speaking Mandarin, Italian, and Croatian in addition to English, and with families with roots in Hong Kong, the Philippines, and Europe, in addition to Canada. Socioeconomic background was high. No children were identified with special needs, as such identification does not happen in this school until the end of Grade 2, to allow for developmental maturity.

Susan was trained to identify concepts that her students must learn, devise learning experiences to teach them, and then evaluate their understanding. As a conscientious Grade 1 teacher, she knew that she was expected to teach the basic concepts of measurement. She organized significant learning experiences in the fall to ensure this. This chapter shares her surprise upon discovering in March that the children revealed a surprising lack of understanding of the very concepts she felt she had so thoroughly taught in the fall. The gap between her teaching and her students' understanding was perplexing (and distressing). She wondered whether conceptual understanding is constructed by the student or acquired from a teacher's teaching?

UNDERSTANDING WHAT CHILDREN MUST UNDERSTAND TO MEASURE

Using Van de Walle (2001), we were considering developmentally appropriate mathematics. His constructivist perspective encourages the mathematical consideration of big ideas. It makes connections between the children's experiences and the philosophical foundations of mathematics. Susan suspected that measuring activities should start with where the children are in their development, but wondered how to pinpoint where the children "are" and how to nurture different stages? Van de Walle (2001) describes how first graders measure length:

> Typically a group of first graders measures the length of their classrooms by laying strips of paper, one meter long, end to end. But the strips overlap, and the line weaves in a snake-like fashion around the desks. Do they understand the concept of length as an attribute of the classroom? Do they understand that each strip of 1m has this attribute of length? Do they understand that their task is to fill smaller units of length into a longer one? What they most likely understand is that they are supposed to be making a line of strips stretching from wall to wall. They are performing a procedure instrumentally, without a concept base. (p. 278)

In spite of how regularly measurement is used in everyday life, results of national and international assessments indicate that North American students are significantly deficient in their knowledge of measurement concepts and skills (Chapin & Johnson, 2000). If such traditional ways of teaching measurement as measuring your classroom are not effective, Susan wondered how else she might help the children. How do the teachers of Reggio Emilia approach mathematics? Susan believed their approach was always authentic and part of a meaningful project.

The process of measuring consists of three seemingly simple steps:

1. Select an attribute to measure
2. Choose a unit of measurement
3. Determine the number of units using a measuring tool

But before this process can begin, children must have developed some basic concepts that cannot be taught: conservation, transitivity, and unit iteration (Van de

Walle, 2001). Instead experiences are needed to give the child a background from which the concepts can develop. Our interpretation of these concepts follows:

Conservation. An object remains the same size even if it is rearranged or transformed. For example, two pencils of equal length remain equal in length when one pencil is placed ahead of the other. Piaget determined that most children grasp conservation of length and area between the ages of 7 to 9 years (Piaget, 1954/1971).

Transitivity. When two objects cannot be compared directly, it is necessary to compare them by means of a third object. For instance, if you were measuring someone's wrist in order to make a bracelet, you could use string or a paper strip as the model for a specific length. Transitivity is the use of a third object, a physical model, when comparing two lengths. Conservation precedes the understanding of transitivity because a child must be sure a tool's length remains the same when it is moved.

Unit iteration. Iteration is the repeated use of the same unit of measurement. Students can lay out many straws across a desk to measure its length or width, but when only one straw is available the unit must be used repeatedly, or iterated, across the desk.

Susan wondered whether teaching a process—like measuring the classroom—without having gained an understanding of the above concepts might lead to misunderstanding? Could she facilitate experiences that would help the children develop an understanding of the concepts, and not simply teach a process?

Susan saw in a jewelry-making project an opportunity for the children to explore measurement meaningfully. Susan watched them use estimation and a trial and error method to determine the lengths of their necklaces, often comparing necklaces against their bodies, either adding or taking away beads to create the right length. She had also noted how the girls were interested in making structures that related to their personal size, ones they could walk under or fit inside. Did this observation connect with Van de Walle's big idea that to develop an understanding of attributes children must make comparisons?

Van de Walle's (2001) idea was that "making other comparisons of an attribute with units produces what is called a measure" (p. 278). Van de Walle claims that making physical models of measuring is useful, so Susan wanted to test this out within the context of the project and challenged the children to make another piece of jewelry, this time for a family member. The children were asked if it would have to be longer or shorter than their own jewelry and if they could find a way to model or show what size was needed. They came back to school clutching pieces of paper, string, and one child even had a paper arm. They compared the new jewelry they were constructing to the pieces of string or paper they brought from home to indicate the required length. They made clay heads of jewelry wearers and again applied the idea of using a physical model of measurement. Once the heads were glazed they added the jewelry, measuring around necks, heads, and ears using a paper strip or piece of string as a guide to ascertain the required length.

UNDERSTANDING WHAT CHILDREN DON'T UNDERSTAND

Susan and Anna used a story as a provocation to invite the children to think about units of measurement, iteration and measuring tools: *How Big Is a Foot?* (Myller, 1990). In this story, a king wants to make a bed for his queen, for her birthday, but cannot figure out what size it needs to be. Susan stopped reading to see if the children could solve the story's problem. A rich class discussion followed, which revealed prior knowledge about terminology such as king-size, queen-size, double, and twin beds as they relate to the attributes of length and width.

> I sleep in a king-size bed and I'm not a king.
> My dad sleeps in a queen-size bed and he fits.
> The bed should be 10 by 5. (Susan asked, "Ten by five what?" but the
>   child was uncertain.)
> The king needs to know how tall and fat the queen is.
> Are they going to let their children into the bed, because then it will have
>   to be bigger.
> He should measure the queen and add a bit extra.
> No, I think the king sleeps with the queen; he needs to add room for
>   himself.
> When dad snores he goes in the spare room; maybe the king snores and
>   doesn't sleep with the queen.
> The queen would fit in my bed.
> No, how do you know she isn't a giant queen? You can't tell from a
>   picture, only if she was here.
> Actually, you need to know the size of the room; my parents got a king-
>   size bed and sent it back because it wouldn't fit through the door.

Once again Susan noticed the children comparing the attribute to be measured to themselves. After a long discussion, measurement was posed as the solution to find out the length and width of the bed. "I know now, it's 10 long ways and 5 short ways."

The children *seemed* to be recognizing the attributes of length and width. Susan finished the story: The king uses his feet to measure the queen. A problem arises when a short apprentice builds the bed and it is too small because his feet are tiny. The apprentice gets thrown in jail but is released when he comes up with the idea of making a plaster cast of the king's foot to use as a measuring tool. The children laughed and seemed to grasp the foolishness of the apprentice, but did they understand how different-size feet could produce different measurements, or did they just think he made a mistake? Did they see the need for a standardized unit of measure? Did they grasp what an adult might see as obvious from the story, or did they have to experience it for themselves?

The children expressed their desire to use their own feet to measure their classroom, objects, and each other, and record their findings. With partners they drew around their feet and used the paper cutouts to measure. Problems arose as they worked with partners and their measurements were different. They seemed puzzled at first, leading Susan to realize they did not fully understand that the

Figure 6.1. Handmade measuring tools.

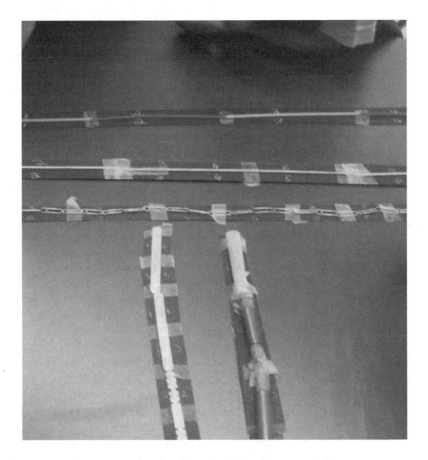

apprentice had smaller feet than the king. They now discovered for themselves that people with small feet have higher measurements and people with large feet have lower measurements. Also, there was overlapping and difficulty in iteration of the unit when an object was large. The paper feet moved and slipped and when measuring each other there were bumps to go over. They could not measure in a straight line. They needed a way to measure with more foot cutouts, they said. So they began to mass-produce paper feet and made individual rulers of feet stuck onto a long strip of cardboard.

They came to the conclusion that a single foot was a good measure for smaller objects but that rulers were good to measure carpets and walls. They saw that measuring tools needed to be of different lengths and identified as to whose feet, and that they needed a flexible tape measure for bodies and curved things. A period of designing rulers out of different objects began—paper clip rulers, crayon rulers, popsicle stick rulers (see Figure 6.1).

Notation also began to appear on the different measuring tools they were inventing. Interesting discussions ensued as the children argued over where the numbers should go. Some rulers had a string of numbers not corresponding to any of the measures on the ruler. Others displayed one-to-one correspondence between the units of measurement and the number but the positioning of the numbers was at the center of the unit. Others followed the conventions of standardized measuring tools with numbers at the end of each unit. Standardized measuring tools were brought in from home and displayed in class. While children who had not considered a relationship between the units of measure and the numbers began to understand and wanted to make new rulers, the children with different positioning stuck to their beliefs, even after consulting standard rulers.

All these varied experiences had encouraged much dialogue, validated their previous experiences, and promoted critical thinking on the topic of measurement. At the end of the term, both Susan and Jennifer, who had been discussing the process with Susan throughout, thought they had really done a good job of teaching measurement.

THE FLOWER BOX PROPOSAL

In March, the class was invited to make a proposal to the student council and asked for some flower boxes for the new playground. Susan and Anna saw the opportunity to revisit measurement and reread *A Pig is Big* (Florian, 2000). This time they wanted the use of literature to be at the right level for the children's understanding. This story deals with a pig that travels widely, noting things that are big, bigger, and biggest. The pig regards the size of everything he sees in relation to himself, just like the children. As Susan read the story and invited the class to estimate the size of the pig, they used their bodies to relate to the size. They said that if it was a piglet it would be tiny:

> This is how tiny a baby pig is. . .
> Well, how big is tiny?
> You don't know until you measure.

Susan reread the documentation from earlier in the year and reminded the students of their experiences making measurement tools. She asked them how they we going to plan the garden boxes and they said they wanted to dig up the butterfly-attracting perennials from their old playground and transplant them into the new boxes. They thought that they would begin by looking at the plants coming up so they would know what size boxes they needed. While Anna remained in the classroom, a small group of five interested children went with Susan to survey the old garden. They took clipboards and paper to draw all the plants they could find, as this would help them decide what size boxes were required. It was spring and new shoots as well as old plants were visible. They began to draw all the plants they could see and planned to transplant. They also counted how many plants were in each of the two flower beds (see Figure 6.2). Susan wondered: "Why is their first thought to *quantify*, not *measure* the space the plants occupy? Are quantifying and comparing common quests of childhood and important when exploring measurement?"

FIGURE 6.2. Girls counting plants in the garden area.

Immediately there were problems as they could not agree on how to count the plants. Everyone had a different total. Several plants had spread and there was the odd new shoot here and there. Some children thought the shoots belonged to the big plant and should not be counted; others said they will grow bigger and should be counted. Now doubt was cast on the whole project. A heated argument erupted and Susan wondered whether to intervene or if they could come to a consensus.

How do we know what size the plants will grow to?
Never mind, we will leave extra space when we have finished counting.

Have the children differentiated between measuring and counting? Are they acknowledging the numerical value of measurement? Susan decided to intervene by asking how counting would help them work out the size of the planters. The strong personalities of the conflicted group stopped trying to get their own count accepted and thought quietly for some time. Had she asked too difficult a question? Then one child smiled triumphantly and said she was fairly sure they needed to make calculations. The rest of the group agreed. They looked more tolerantly this time at everyone's numbers and decided to discard the lowest counts—"because the plants will get bigger so we need the biggest number." Susan thought it amazing how arguments and conflicts could be so heated with no one backing down and then how quickly they could accommodate another opinion as they rethought their ideas. The children never acknowledged this change of mind, nor did they seem upset when a more plausible way forward was proposed by one of their peers. Susan wondered whether they could accept correction more easily from a peer than a teacher. After looking carefully at everyone's clipboard they arrived at a total of 16 plants:

> These are too many for one box, we need two boxes so we have to put some plants in each.
> Let's find out all the ways of making 16 so we know what we can put in each one.

They worked out all the possible combinations of 16 and returned triumphantly to the class to tell the others.

Susan, on the other hand, was wondering what would happen next and if she was experienced enough to be trying this. Why were they still counting and not measuring? Where was she going wrong as a facilitator? Should she try to mention size or measurement or would they arrive at it in their in own time? Is the idea of area or even the recognition of lengths and widths too difficult for them? Susan thought about all the brilliant things she had done around the jewelry project to teach measurement and wondered if this revisiting was leading anywhere.

Back in the classroom, the children explained their work to the large group. They read out their list of all the possible combinations of 16. "Well, we could have $0 + 16 = 16$, $15 + 1 = 16$, $14 + 2 \ldots$." They were interrupted and greeted with incredulity: "You're crazy. Why would you put 15 plants in one box and one in another? This isn't right. You need to cross those out." Reluctantly, they went through the list and discarded all but the two equations ($8 + 8 = 16$ and $9 + 7 = 16$) that the class found reasonable. The discussion resumed: "How do you know 16 plants will fit in two boxes anyway? You might need three or four boxes."

Unwilling to be totally discredited they reply:

> Well, of course I meant two very big boxes, not tiny boxes.
> What do you mean big and tiny? We have to see what the store has. If they have tiny we need lots. If they have big ones, maybe only two.
> We need to measure, but what shall we measure? The boxes in the store? Shall we visit the store or measure the plants?
> Both! Let's measure the plants first because they are here. We need to see how tall they are. We could measure with our pencil tool.
> But there are roots and we need to see how deep they go.
> Roots can go sideways. We need to measure, up, down and sideways. (She uses her body to show the directions of the roots.)
> But there are two sideways. One this way and one that way. (She points right and left.)
> Okay, we will measure up, down, and two sideways. What shall we use?

No, wait a minute. That's not all. There's up, down, and all the way
round sideways. It's a circle around the plant.
We have to measure what's inside the box and what's inside the
measuring lines around the plant.
A circle is flat. We have to measure more. (Susan wonders if this "more"
was referring to volume.)
We could dig up the plants and fill the holes with bricks. If we count the
bricks we know how much space the plant needs.

It was the end of the school day and we had to stop. This discussion had taken
a long time, and they had only just arrived at the notion of measurement. They
finally verbalized in their own words that plants have the attributes of height,
width, and breadth ("sideways all around") to measure. They were wondering
whether they needed volume or area. Did they realize a relationship exists between linear measurements and volume? Can they solve this dilemma?

The Dilemma of Uncertainty

Susan was totally unsure how to begin the next day. She felt very unsettled.
After discussion with Jennifer and Anna, they decided to reread their conversations to the children. The children, however, seemed much more confident, purposeful, and determined to solve the problem. Anna suggested digging up a plant
to look at, as a visual aid to thinking. Susan began with a small group of five
children. One from the previous day preferred another activity, and another child
joined the group, her interest piqued by the documentation review. Susan showed
them the dug-up plant. They carefully examined it and said, "It's not a circle we
need to measure. It's a cylinder." They rushed to get the geometric solids box to
compare the 3-D cylinder with the plant roots. Again Susan noted this need for a
physical comparison and model. They wanted to draw the plant and mark where
they would measure before they went out to the garden. They drew lines showing
the height and width, and a circle to denote the three-dimensional aspect of the
root measurement. They looked carefully at each other's measurement plans and
decided to use the clearest one. After this planning stage they considered what
they needed, collected their homemade measuring tools (the straw and pencil rulers), the chosen plan, and headed for the garden with Susan.

The first plant they saw was a creeper that hugs the ground. "Damn", said
one child, as she looked at her long straw ruler and the almost flat plant. They
stared at the plant in disbelief. Then a child had an idea and ran back to the class
for something, returning with a box of tiles to place on top of the plant (see Figure 6.3).

They proceeded from plant to plant, covering the areas of short plants with
tiles, and measuring the length of tall ones with their tools and sticks. They generated a list of measures in straws, pencils, and tiles, and wondered:

What do we do now?
We add them all together, I think.

FIGURE 6.3. Using tiles to compare area of plants outside.

Yes, but there's too many numbers, we need a calculator.
Yes, but we can't add them because they're all different.
No, they're all plants.
Yes, but straw, tiles, and pencils are different. You can only add the same thing.

(They looked dispirited and wondered what to do next.)
I know. Let's measure them all again with tiles.
But what about the tall ones?
Let's measure under the tall tree ones, around where the branches would
    be if they were on the ground. The top of the tree won't be in the
    flower box, we don't need the tall bit.

They worked hard remeasuring with the tiles and listed their measurements for 16 plants. They returned to class, and explained that they had had a measuring plan that didn't work but that they had solved the problem with tiles. They told the class about measuring in different units and how they couldn't add them up. They displayed their list of tile measurements and asked who could add them on the calculator. The class chose two volunteers who could be trusted to add accurately on the calculator.

The next day the same small group watched their list of measurements being added up with a calculator. Our calculator experts gave them a running commentary on how to use a calculator. They reached a total area of 157 tiles and were very impressed. The group of five children from the previous day then resumed ownership of the task:

We need to see how much this is.
Let's put the tiles on the carpet and mark out 157 tiles so we know how
    big it is.
(They begin to place the tiles on the carpet and soon run out of tiles.)
We can move the first row!

This student demonstrated that the unit could be iterated, and they continued laboriously until they reached 157. They marked out the area on the rug with masking tape and then estimated how many planters would fit into the designated space. They called a class meeting so everyone could look at the area they had found (see Figure 6.4).

Collaborating with Others

The school grounds are the responsibility of Mr. Dan, who was invited to class to see the wonderful area of 157 tiles taped out on the carpet. The children asked him about their budget and the best place to buy planters. He returned with a catalog of planters of all shapes, sizes, and materials for the children to choose from. A group of four volunteers compared the size of the catalog planters with the demarcated carpet area. As the catalog used standard units, they chose standardized measuring rulers and taped out the area of the planters on top of our marked area for plants. They could fit three boxes into the area with a small area not covered. They discussed the leftover area that was not big enough for a fourth box, and ideas of rounding up and down and approximation were considered. But they did not seem to mind this leftover area: "One of the plants was a bit brown. We'll leave that one behind." Nor did they mind the fact they had made calculations earlier based on two boxes.

FIGURE 6.4. Flower box area in tiles on the carpet inside.

Throughout the next day everyone had a chance to look at the pictures, sizes, and prices, and make a personal choice. At the end of the day, we listed the possibilities and a vote was taken. Three terracotta-colored plastic flower boxes were ordered. Mr. Dan received constant inquiries up until the time of their arrival. The morning they arrived there was such great excitement in the room. It was quite remarkable that the children would regard them so highly. Bags of earth were delivered as well, and the children could not wait to begin transplanting. Susan wondered whether they viewed the pots and earth as the culmination of so much hard work.

The flower boxes were laid on the carpet to ensure the correct area was covered, and at morning meeting they considered suitable sites in the playground for the planters. They decided they needed to observe the sun for a whole day so they could pick the sunniest spots. They were also concerned about water. Two children volunteered to monitor the sun every hour throughout the day and report to the class. A different group of five went out to survey the playground for water taps. Problems arose as they thought the boxes should be spaced out along a sunny wall, but this would mean one box was very far from the water tap. They returned to class and consulted a catalog again for the lengths of garden hoses available. Measurements were given in meters but they wanted to measure from the water tap to the furthest box with their homemade rulers, so outside we went to begin measuring again.

The following day it was raining, and at morning meeting the class convinced the small group they could not measure in straws but needed to use the standard wooden meter stick, like they did for the boxes. "Anything from the books [catalogs] needs the wooden teachers' rulers." One child suggested seeing how many straws fit into a meter stick, but time was short. They were so eager to begin digging, they decided it was quicker to remeasure the length of hose required by using the meter stick. "Besides, the rain will ruin your rule, it's better to mess up the school one. Wood is stronger, it will just get muddy, and we can wipe it off. Yours is paper, it will be wrecked." The same group of five children insisted on braving the rain and measured with a meter stick. At the end of the day they shared this measurement and talked about purchasing a hose for the flower boxes.

The children contacted Mr. Dan and learned that they had spent the budget available. "Why don't we use the watering can and water the plants when we go out for recess. We can take it in turns." They were not the least bothered that they had spent 2 days measuring and had to give up on the hose. When they recognized a good solution, they could accept it.

Everyone wanted a turn digging up and transplanting the plants, so teams of diggers and planters and watering can helpers were worked out. Susan and Anna took turns escorting groups with spades and buckets to dig up the plants and carry them to the new playground. Other groups took over filling the boxes with soil and planting. The watering groups were happy because there was so much soil spilled that they got the additional job of sweeping up before watering. The plants were transplanted, watered, and carefully tended by the children.

TEACHER REFLECTIONS

For Susan, as facilitator, it was difficult and uncomfortable not to know which direction the project was going, or how much guidance to give, or when to intervene with a question. Yet, even when Susan was doubtful that the children could resolve problems, they proved themselves to be intellectually powerful. Also significant was the realization that as teachers we are colearners with the children, investigating how they learn. This realization helped Susan and her colleagues through the learning process. Collaboration among Susan, Jennifer, and Anna was helpful to the construction of Susan's own ideas.

Documentation

Documentation was essential to the emergence of this project. The fact that Susan and Anna had documented earlier observations and understandings in the jewelry project meant they had a trace of learning to compare with the later measurement experiences. At the beginning of their Reggio investigation Susan and Anna tended to document everything and ended up with an excessive and overwhelming amount of dialogue and observations. As they became more comfortable with emergent curriculum and facilitation of projects, however, they learned to be more discerning. There were moments in this project that were valuable but not recorded simply because it was not always possible to do so. Some conversations were recorded at length only for the team to realize they did not contribute much to their ideas or to the children's learning or they were not helpful in propelling the project further. Much of what was documented is not included here but provided a choice of observations to consider and was needed on a day-to-day basis to help the children and teachers revisit their thinking and probe deeper into problem solving. While the documentation would be too much to present here in its entirety, it helped Susan and Anna to use learning experiences for multiple purposes. Initially it helped propel projects forward and assisted teacher understanding not merely of the mathematical journey but also of social and emotional development, as well as children's ability to converse, to reason, and to speak before an audience. Later, documentation aided in presenting these experiences to parents and other audiences, such as educators at conferences.

Documentation is diagnostic, both a formative and summative assessment of the children's learning. As Susan wrote her report cards, she found herself quoting from their ideas in projects as evidence of their learning. The documentation helped some parents see their children's abilities in a different light and prompted many conversations about projects and how the children were interested in using measurement at home, investigating their father's tool box or measuring family members.

Strength in Children

Some students in the class might have been considered weak in mathematics had they been assessed using only traditional methods, but they excelled when involved in this garden project. For example, one child would become visibly distressed when asked to think about large numbers over 20, yet she was the one who counted out the tiles to 157 with much perseverance and enthusiasm when she had peer support and a purpose for accomplishing the task. She showed us that "all children have preparedness, potential, curiosity, and interest in constructing their learning" (Gandini, 1993, p. 5).

Collaboration

Continuous professional dialogue throughout the year among Susan, Jennifer, and Anna contributed to an understanding of the learning processes taking place. Susan and Jennifer met once a week, with Jennifer consistently provoking Susan to think about what Van de Walle would say concerning the observations Susan brought to the meeting. Susan would bring her data and think the children did not understand, and Jennifer would see the situation differently and sometimes suggest other tacks to try. In this rhythm of sharing and response, Jennifer prodded Susan to "mine" the documentation on the jewelry project to study the children's mathematical thinking. Susan believes her understanding of the concepts of measurement has increased, and she is beginning to see the benefit of documentation, not simply as a trace of children's learning but as professional development for the teachers involved. She said, "The most perplexing and ultimately enticing problem that emerged was recognition that as educators we tend to overestimate our students' academic ability and underestimate their intellectual capabilities." The final flower boxes, resplendent with flowers, are not the only cause for celebration of this project; the flowers in their boxes remind us of the ambiguous, amazing journey of thinking, motivation, and learning from inquiry for both children and teachers.

CAROL ANNE'S COMMENTS

Susan suggests that perhaps counting is such a "common quest" in childhood that it is an automatic response before other processes can occur. She shows us a teacher thinking very carefully about children's understanding, a teacher who shows courage in confronting a discomfiting fact—that what appeared to be taught and learned in the fall did not seem to hold in April. And she shows impressive restraint in not interfering in the trajectory of the girls' thought when they begin to count plants instead of measuring. She merely asks a question. The girls thus do not feel corrected and are able to continue thinking. Even though the small group presented counting algorithms to the class when they returned inside, collaborative discussion brought the group to agreement that measuring was necessary. Susan and Jennifer help us see the fluidity in learning, the slow construction of understanding, its unevenness across a group and across time, and the ways a child with an idea can lead peers.

To me this chapter is particularly noteworthy for two ways that the teacher's study of children's learning is supported. One is through the documentation, which enables Susan to think repeatedly about the children's mathematical understanding. The documentation is in the background in this chapter, yet is a supportive structure to teacher thinking. The other is the opportunity to discuss mathematical understanding in depth with her principal, Jennifer, and to share their thoughts as a pedagogy of listening to the children. In this second section of the book, highlighting long-term efforts in emergent curriculum, it is intriguing to watch for the ways teachers listen to children.

CHAPTER 7

Children's Conversations About the Sun, Moon, and Earth

Brenda Jacobs

What would 5-year-olds find interesting about Cannon's story *Stellaluna* (1993)? Our emergent curriculum project took place in an afternoon kindergarten class in a public school that follows a standardized curriculum (Ministry of Education and Training, 1998a). The six boys and girls who were the main "protagonists" had a range of academic abilities and social skills, and came from diverse racial or ethnic backgrounds (such as White, Black, and Chinese). Kari was a natural leader, always able to get the other children on board with her ideas. She and Kaitlin were the best of friends, and I enjoyed watching how the girls collaborated with each other. Another girl, Jaeda, enjoyed working on the aesthetic components of the project. Camille had the strongest literacy skills of all the children in the group. Harry had recently come to Canada from China and was just learning to speak English. We all liked his enthusiastic, gregarious nature. Gabriel was the youngest member of the group, confident, popular, and mature beyond his years. While the other children in the class went to gym, library, or music, these children met with me for a total of 35 sessions over 4 months, their enthusiasm and excitement continuing until the end of the year. Having studied the Reggio Emilia approach, I was trying out an emergent curriculum in my own setting to see if I could make it work.

Emergent curriculum starts with a provocation introduced by a child, teacher, parent, or members of the community. A provocation can be an idea, an event, or an object that captures the children's imagination and desire to learn more. Children become aware of their own ability to think, aware that they have their own opinions and theories, and understand that through dialogue they continue to build their own knowledge. They become protagonists of their own learning. The teacher facilitates and provides an environment that enables the children to choose from a variety of learning possibilities that are exciting and challenging. Such curriculum is more meaningful because it is based in the children's own interests. It provides opportunities for children's learning to far exceed what is listed in the expectations of standardized curriculum.

Our project began with a conversation to search for an interesting research question after we read Cannon's (1993) story about bats and birds. I was thinking of Gallas's idea of "structured dialogue" (1995) where children coconstruct ideas about questions through dialogue. This process allows children to have a sense of control over their learning. When teachers listen to their students' conversations without interrupting, we see that the process of collaboration has the potential to teach us what children are thinking. It gives educators the opportunity to see how children's ideas develop and how theories are built, and to be impressed by the power of children thinking together.

Like Cadwell (2003), I began with an entry point into the dialogue that allowed the children to lead the conversation and to have a number of possible choices about the content and form. In retrospect, it was the first time I had ever had a conversation with young children where I truly facilitated it rather than dominating or trying to control it. I audiotaped and transcribed all our conversations, and at each session I shared with the children our previous conversation. This revisiting of the documented conversation enabled the children to reflect on what they had said in previous sessions and motivated further questions and interest in the project. It also helped us plan further activities. I also took digital photos and shared them with the children. This made revisiting previous conversations more meaningful because the photographs supported the conversation on the transcription. At the end of the project, we decided to write a story about what we had done and put it onto panels with the other documentation. After the panels were made, the parents were invited to a presentation by the children to hear and see what their children had been learning about.

I found that both Gallas' (1995) and Cadwell's (2003) work helped me understand where to begin the project, but it was reading about an extensive number of Reggio Emilia projects, such as *Ring-around-the-Rosie* (Giudici et al., 2001) that helped me sustain it. Prior to our first conversation, I made some initial predictions about the project that the children were going to undertake in order to clarify my own understanding of the strategies I would use. My predictions were based on possibilities of what might happen and were a reflection of the children's current interests in the classroom. After each session, I transcribed and reviewed the documentation in order to understand and interpret our conversation. After reflecting on these materials, I would consider other possible ideas and directions for the continuation of the project the following session. I believe that revisiting the documentation is very important because it modifies teacher thoughts and predictions about interactions with the children. It also makes visible the interweaving of the actions of children and adults. It helped the children reflect on their own understanding, share their knowledge of the project question, and see how much they had learned as the project progressed.

A STORY AS STARTING POINT

The first time the children and I met, I explained to them that we were going to start with a conversation to find an interesting question we all wanted to learn more about. I asked the children if there was anything about the story *Stellaluna* (Cannon, 1993) that they found interesting:

> *Kari:* She slept at night and she didn't sleep in the morning.
> *Harry:* Birds can see in the night.
> *Brenda:* Can birds see in the night?
> *Harry:* No, only bats.

They made initial hypotheses about daytime, nighttime, and the movement of the sun, moon, and earth:

> *Harry:* In Canada it's night and in China it's morning, I think maybe sun, maybe the moon, around and around and around.
> *Gabriel:* The sun goes to the other side of the world when it's night in Canada.
> *Camille:* The moon comes out … the moon goes around the other side of the sun.
> *Kari:* The sun goes to the other side of the world when it's morning in Canada, and when it's night in Canada it's morning in the other half of the world, and when it's morning in Canada it is night on the other side of the world.

Throughout the conversation the parameters of the dialogue continued to widen, but there was an internal logic, and at the end of the conversation they had come full circle and once again talked about bats:

> *Camille:* One time when I was at the cottage with my friends I saw a real bat flying in the air.
> *Jaeda:* Why do bats sleep in the morning and they be awake in the dark?

During our second session, I revisited what we had talked about in our first session by reading various parts of the transcription aloud to the children. I found this way of starting each session worthwhile, as it gave the children a chance to reflect on what we had done previously, helped refresh their memories, and helped any children who had been absent, enabling them to catch up on what they had missed. The children were always amazed and delighted that their words had been recorded and were so valued! I reminded the children that they needed to come up with a question about something they all wanted to learn about so that we could plan what we wanted to do next. The children came up with three possible questions. Surprisingly, the children's initial comments about morning and night became the focus of the research group, as together they decided on the question "Why is it dark at nighttime and light in the morning?" I then asked them how they thought we should start the project, and someone suggested we go to the library. We talked about how we all had different ideas about whether the sun, moon, and earth move or if they stay still.

PREDICTING WHAT TO DRAW

The children decided that they wanted to make a drawing so that they could record their own thoughts about the movement of the sun, moon, and earth because they all had different ideas in their heads. Once they had an idea of what they were going to draw, I wanted them to come to me and predict what they thought their pictures were going to look like. The predictions represented what the children were thinking at that moment in time about the sun, moon, and earth. The significance of exploring the children's initial predictions is that this provided me with a sense of how their thinking changed over the course of the project.

While working on their first pencil drawings, the children shared their ideas with each other about the size of the sun. The following example shows how the children were able to enrich their own knowledge through the knowledge of others:

> *Kari:* That's the sun.
> *Kaitlin:* Do you know what it is made from? I think it is made from fire.
> *Gabriel:* Actually, the sun is this big.
> *Harry:* The sun is *this* big.
> *Gabriel:* You're right Harry, but for us it is small because we live farther from the sun, but for astronauts when they are in space it is big.

I thought Gabriel was thinking about why his and Harry's suns were different sizes. Gabriel was taking the perspective of how the sun looks to us from earth and suggested that Harry's perspective was of the sun seen in space. Gabriel understood this difference and was even able to articulate this concept clearly to Harry.

Many of the children drew exactly what they predicted, and others made changes as they went along. When the children had finished their first pencil drawings, I asked them to describe their pictures to the rest of the group. While the children shared their work, they compared their pictures and realized that there were differences. They were puzzled about why some children had drawn the sun bigger than the earth while others had drawn the earth bigger than the sun. This difference sparked interesting discussion that nurtured ideas and contributed to group knowledge:

> *Kaitlin:* My world is the biggest, then Kari's, then Jaeda's. I did mine smaller than the earth because, well, you can tell.
> *Jaeda* (referring to Kaitlin's picture): The sun is smaller.
> *Kari:* And the sun in Harry's picture is huge.
> *Jaeda:* How is it huge?
> *Brenda:* Well, it took up a lot of his paper. The whole side, wasn't it, Kari?
> *Kari:* The whole side.
> *Jaeda:* Harry's sun was big.

Jaeda tried to figure out the difference between her sun being the biggest and Harry's being huge. I asked the children how we could find out whether the sun was bigger than the earth. Kari and Kaitlin seemed convinced that the earth is the biggest (see Figure 7.1).

Jaeda was still convinced the sun is the biggest, and suggested that the birds can see the sun even bigger from up in the sky. The children wondered how we could check which one really is the biggest and decided to look at the books from the library. Jaeda confidently said, "I'm definitely right, the sun is bigger," and

FIGURE 7.1. Kari's first drawing shows the earth larger than the sun. She shows daytime on the sun side and nighttime on the moon side.

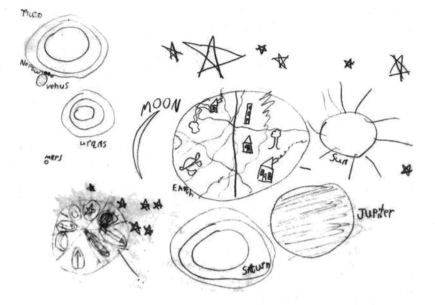

Kari agreed, "The sun is the biggest: the moon is puny."

When the children compared their pictures they realized that they had different ideas about how planets spin in space and their movement (orbits) through space. The discussion focused on the idea of movement and how the moon goes around the earth and the earth goes around the sun. We talked about how nothing goes around the moon. When I discussed each picture with each child, Jaeda told me that she would use arrows to show the earth spinning:

> *Jaeda:* I showed how the earth turns by putting arrows.
> *Brenda:* Where is your moon? (Jaeda points.) So is the moon going around the earth in your picture?
> *Jaeda:* Yeah.
> *Brenda:* How could you show the direction of the moon?
> *Jaeda* (pointing to the moon and dragging her finger around the earth): If I put a line like that.
> *Brenda:* Is your moon going around your earth, Camille?
> *Camille:* No, they are staying in one place.

As the children shared their ideas with each other, they started to think about how they would change their pictures based on the knowledge they were gaining from others in the group. For example, they tried to help one another think about how to show the change from daytime to nighttime in their pictures:

> *Harry:* We can ___ here. (Harry used his hand to show two halves of the earth.)

Brenda: Look what Harry is doing, Gabriel, he is just thinking about how
     he can show it is sunny on one side of the earth and not on the other.
Harry: Cut it … hum.
Brenda: Instead of cutting it what can he do?
Gabriel: Draw a line.

Even though Harry did not draw a line on his earth to show the difference between night and day, he understood that by drawing it he could show the sunny
and dark side of the earth. He was having difficulty expressing his idea in English,
but Gabriel understood exactly what Harry meant.

Kari too had her own idea about how to show daytime and nighttime in her
picture. She drew a line separating the earth in half and said, "Because when the
sun is on this side, it is sunny on this side. And when it is sunny on this side, it is
not sunny on this side." I confirmed this by asking, "Is that the nighttime side and
the other side is the daytime side?" Kari agreed, "Yeah."

DRAMATIZING THE MOTION OF PLANETS

At this point, I felt that the children needed the opportunity to orient themselves
in physical space in a way that might represent what they had drawn in their
first pencil drawings. I hoped that by moving from two-dimensional drawing
to a three-dimensional drama experience, their thinking about the project question would be further enhanced. I brought a flashlight and globe to school for
the children to use to aid their drama of the movement of the sun, moon and
earth. The children spun the globe and I shone the flashlight on it. They noticed
that the light was not always shining on the same place. We talked about how
daytime is where the light shines on the globe and nighttime is where it was not
shining. I asked the children who would like to be the sun, the earth, and the
moon. Gabriel chose to be the earth, and as he spun and rotated around the sun,
I told the children that when the earth rotates around the sun, we say it "orbits."
Even though I had avoided giving the children any information like this so far in
the project, I felt the word *orbit* would help make things clearer for them when
they were doing the drama. I thought there would be less confusion about the
difference between spinning and orbiting. The children took turns being the sun,
moon, and earth while their peers helped them think about how they would
move in space.

During the drama activity the rest of the group and I were the audience. Our
job was to watch and share our ideas about how the sun and the moon and the
earth travel in space:

Gabriel (spinning the globe): By making the earth turn.
Kari: Walk around. (Kari points to show Gabriel the direction he should
     move in. Gabriel follows around the sun.)
Brenda: Camille, go and show us what the moon should do. (Camille
     hesitates.)

> *Kaitlin:* I think I know. I think Camille should go behind the back [behind the sun].
> *Kari:* I know, I know! When Gabriel walks around the sun, Camille will walk around Gabriel. Camille, you go beside Gabriel, and Gabriel walks around the sun, and Camille. . .
> *Jaeda:* . . . walks around Gabriel. (The three children start to dramatize the movement but have difficulty with how fast they should go.)

What was most interesting to me was the way that Kari became the "expert" during this conversation. Conceptually, Kari understood the basic relation of sun, moon, and earth in space. Gabriel was clearly stuck when it came to representing the earth going around the sun, and without Kari there to help him think it through he would not have been able to dramatize it. Kari also helped out by saying that Camille should walk around Gabriel. Kari had an amazing capacity to map her conceptual understanding onto the movements of the children.

PREDICTING A SECOND TIME

The children decided that they would like to draw a picture of the sun, moon, and earth again because they would now draw their pictures differently from the way they had the first time. When it was time for the children to predict how their second pencil drawing would be different from their first, it became clear to me that their thinking about the relative size of the sun, moon, and earth in relation to each other had changed. All six children clearly stated now that the sun was largest, the earth was middle-sized, and the moon was the smallest. I also felt that the children's thinking about planetary motion had become more complex because the drama activity had exposed them to different perspectives. When sharing their second pictures, their ideas of how to show movement were now more sophisticated. The children drew the moon traveling around the earth and the earth traveling around the sun.

The children then shared what they had drawn in their second pencil drawings. This time they noticed more similarities than differences among their pictures and they added to or changed part of their own drawing if they wanted. The examples below show an evolution of the children's thinking:

> *Brenda:* Is that your moon, Kari? Is it traveling in the same direction?
> (Kari nods yes. Everyone else in the group confirms that their moon is traveling in the same direction.)
> *Brenda:* Is that your earth, Kari?
> *Kari:* Ring around the Rosie, the sun. (Kari moves her finger in the direction the earth moves.)

Similarly, when sharing their pictures, the children's ideas about how to show nighttime and daytime were more developed:

> *Gabriel:* A line. One part's light, and one part's dark. (He shows daytime and nighttime.)
>
> *Kari:* That's what I did too. It's nighttime on this side, since you see all the nighttime stuff on this side, and it's morning here.

Through collaborative effort, Gabriel and Kari became the "experts" and were sharing their thinking with the rest of the group. The other children in the group learned from them how they represented daytime and nighttime visually in their picture. This example also supports Gardner's (1999) contention that when educators use varied entry points to learning, such as drawing and drama, this strategy enables different children within learning groups to be the "expert."

DISCOVERING THE POWER RELATIONS IN GROUPS

The children wanted to do something bigger with color to show how things move in space. They worked with partners and used their second pencil drawings as guidelines to draw the sun, earth, and moon on large pieces of black construction paper, calling these their "black space pictures." This was quite a difficult task for the children as they had to combine their ideas with a partner's and negotiate what they were going to draw. We talked about the color of the sun and the moon and we thought about what color the earth would be if we were looking at it from space. The children used pastels to color in their outlines and later added black pastel to fill in all the areas around the planets and stars, even though the paper was black already. The children thought this made the pictures look very dark, just like it really is in space. They decided to use white paper and pencil crayons or markers to draw arrows to show how the sun, moon, and earth spin and how the earth and moon orbit. They cut out the arrows and glued them on their pictures.

While working on their black space picture, Camille and Jaeda provided me with an illustration of the difficulties of group work in spite of its benefits for intellectual learning. As I observed their efforts in class, it appeared that they were working cooperatively and productively. I was shocked when I listened to the audiotape. In the following exchange, Camille is trying to engage Jaeda in a conversation by appealing to Jaeda's taste in colors. Jaeda has previously said many times that yellow is her favorite color.

> *Camille:* Someone needs to help me, I can't choose. I think the yellow one is nice. Do you like yellow?
>
> *Jaeda:* No.
>
> Camille (confused): You don't like yellow?
>
> *Jaeda:* No.
>
> *Camille:* You don't like yellow, yellow's not your favorite color?
>
> *Jaeda:* No.
>
> *Camille:* Okay.
>
> *Jaeda:* Only for the sun.

Jaeda and Camille continued to have difficulty, with Jaeda provoking Camille, and drawing Harry into her side of the conversation.

> *Jaeda:* Oooh, I draw scribbly.
> *Camille:* I love to scribble.
> *Jaeda:* Oooh, I don't like scribbles.
> *Harry:* Me neither.
> *Camille:* I love scribbles, it's the best thing in the world when you're drawing.
> *Jaeda:* No, it's not the best kind of drawing. I like perfect drawing.
> *Harry:* And me neither.
> *Jaeda* (to Harry): You like scribbling drawing?
>   *Harry:* No, I like perfect drawing.
> *Jaeda* (directed to Camille): See? See, he's on my side.
> *Camille:* I like scribbling when concentrating. I'm a fancy scribbler.

Camille became more and more uncomfortable as the discussion continued and out of desperation said she didn't like scribbling anymore. Then this:

> *Camille:* Look what kind of scissors I have.
> *Jaeda:* What kind of scissors do you have? They do zigzags, I like perfect scissors that doesn't have zigzags. Do you like zigzags [to Harry]?
> *Harry:* Me neither.
> Camille (pleading): I want to be with you too, Jaeda.
> *Jaeda:* But Harry is in my club. You're part of scribbling, and we don't.
> *Harry:* Yeah.
> Jaeda (turning to Camille): Do you like scribbling?
> Camille (defeated): No.
> *Jaeda:* Okay, it is not scribbling club, whoever scribbles. . .
> *Camille:* Jaeda, stop talking!
> *Jaeda:* Okay.
> *Harry:* Yup, stop talking!

At this point, I had come over to check on the group and had no idea that this conversation had occurred. Whenever I had looked over, it appeared as if the group was working together cooperatively and productively. Conversations like these could marginalize Camille. On the other hand, as we can see from a photo of them creating their black space picture (see Figure 7.2), their relationship includes closeness and ease of working together, in spite of the verbal conflict.

Kari and Kaitlin also had differences of opinion, but their relationship provides an example of how children can communicate effectively and deal positively with each other when working through tensions collaboratively. This example shows how children negotiate with others to build a jointly shared knowledge base. During their initial conversations, I could see that there was a very strong bond between the two girls. They were at ease with one another and had a natural rhythm in how they communicated. They were negotiating where to draw on the paper, what to draw, and who should draw what.

FIGURE 7.2. Working together on black space pictures.

> *Kari:* I'm going to do the sun.
> *Kaitlin:* Make sure it's huge!
> *Kari:* A space man is right there, there's a space man.
> *Kaitlin:* Let's do lots of space men, and space girls.
> *Kari:* And look, it's a star person sitting on a couch made of moon cheese,
>   the cheese from the moon. (She laughs!)
> *Kaitlin:* When she's hungry, she just breaks little pieces off.
> *Kari:* When she gets hungry, she just breaks the cheese off the couch.

I think Kaitlin wanted to draw the sun but in the end she just gave Kari advice that it should be huge. Kari drew a space man and Kaitlin added to the idea by suggesting that they do lots of space men, and space girls too. The last part of the exchange was very imaginative. Kaitlin added to Kari's idea of the couch made of moon cheese by suggesting that, when the star person is hungry, she just break little pieces off to eat. Kari brought the idea together by suggesting that the pieces be broken off the couch. We can see from this exchange how the girls shared their ideas, and there was excitement and positive energy in their collaboration.

In the following exchange, Kaitlin tried to figure out a way she could help with the sun (here scribbling is perceived in a positive way):

> *Kaitlin:* Do you want me to do the waves around the sun?
> *Kari:* You do the scribbling of the sun and I'll do the waves.
> *Kaitlin:* Do you want me to do that? (Kaitlin demonstrates.)
> *Kari:* But do it softly, I'll do the fire.

As the conversation unfolded, Kari and Kaitlin continued to negotiate their ideas.

> *Kaitlin:* Do you want the earth to be right here?
> *Kari:* No, it has to be like right here. No, but a little farther that way, not this way, or it will burn up, right?
> *Kaitlin:* Is that big enough?
> *Kari:* That could be the moon.
> *Kaitlin:* OK.
> *Kari:* Let's do the big sun right here. I mean the moon.
> *Kaitlin:* I think that's the earth.

Although Kari didn't tell Kaitlin that her circle was too small to represent the earth, she was helpful by suggesting it be the moon instead. Even when Kaitlin was inquiring where to draw the moon, Kari offered her a logical explanation about why it shouldn't be too close to the sun. Kari was definitely encouraging Kaitlin to think through her ideas, and Kaitlin respected and followed helpful suggestions. Kaitlin could also assert herself, as she corrected Kari about the earth. When these two children worked together in their productive, harmonious way, to me their conversation demonstrated the validity of Vygotsky's (1978) "zone of proximal development" and Malaguzzi's (1998) principle of "circularity." Both concepts point out that what a child is capable of doing on his or her own is enhanced by collaborating with capable peers.

This is not to say that highly productive groups don't have misunderstandings and disagreements, but in these groups the children deal with them in a more positive way. Disagreements and misunderstandings can often be part of a powerful learning experience. In the following exchange, Kari and Kaitlin have a disagreement about the color of the sun. I think this is a good illustration of how a disagreement can encourage children to think things through and come up with an amicable solution (see Figure 7.3).

> *Kari:* Don't color the outline, the outline is going to be orange.
> *Kaitlin:* I kind of forgot that a little.
> *Kari:* That's a shooting star right?
> *Kaitlin:* That guy's going to be orange. I'm going to, like, do a little bit of yellow.
> *Kari:* No, don't do that.
> *Kaitlin:* The whole thing can be yellow and orange, everything until there can be orange.
> Kari (crossly): You can't help any more ever again.
> *Kaitlin:* I don't have to. I know! Your side can be all orange and my side can be orange and yellow. Then it will look a bit prettier.

FIGURE 7.3. Working together on black space pictures.

Kari: No, it won't!
Kaitlin: How about we do it mostly yellow?
Kari (excitedly): We could do it yellow and then do orange over top to
        make it a light orange.
Kaitlin: That's a good idea. (See Figure 7.4.)

At this point, Kaitlin was relieved the difficulty was resolved and came to tell me about it.

Rankin (1997) emphasized that collaboration involves a sense of reciprocity and community among the participants and that different participants take the lead at different times. It is a system of social relationships where children coordinate their actions and change their point of view in relation to each other. These relationships of trust allow for disagreement and conflict. The children communicate effectively among themselves and deal with each other in a positive manner. In such groups I found that children listened to each other, offered constructive advice, complimented each other's efforts, negotiated who should do what, and compromised with each other. They found amicable resolutions to disagreements, encouraged each other to take risks, shared their expertise and knowledge, helped each other in concrete ways, took responsibility for their mistakes, and showed pride in their accomplishments.

TEACHER REFLECTIONS

Since this emergent curriculum project, I am increasingly confident about starting and sustaining projects. Emergent curriculum projects are the part of my teaching that excites me the most. Emergent curriculum works because it is based on the children's own interests and is more meaningful to them because they share control over the content of their learning. It provides opportunities for children's

FIGURE 7.4. Kaitlin and Kari's black space picture shows a huge spinning sun, the earth orbiting the sun, and a tiny crescent moon orbiting the earth. Fat, short arrows indicate orbits and longer arrows show spinning direction. The girls devised this notation system themselves.

learning to far exceed what is listed in the expectations of a standardized curriculum. I teach the expectations, yet I do as much of it as I can through project work. It was scary to venture into the unknown and embrace in practice what I had learned in theory. The best way to incorporate an emergent curriculum project in your classroom is to read how other people have done it, think it through carefully, and just get started. You need to trust in your own knowledge about teaching and trust that the children will lead you into unique and exciting learning experiences that allow everyone to thrive.

CAROL ANNE'S COMMENTS

Brenda's story shows that when children are permitted to ask their own questions, their genuine questions turn out to be astonishing. Who would think kindergarten children could be intrigued by the relative size and motion of the sun, moon, and earth for 4 months? Certainly such a topic could not be imposed on them. Children's own questions are at the leading edge of their development. When teachers use them as a guide to curriculum, they generate motivation. Such questions are a reminder that the quality of children's thinking and work is highest when they take ownership of it. When Brenda lets them suggest what to do, their ownership of the project sustains momentum. The questions her children chose is a reminder that we see the highest quality work children are capable of when they are given control.

We also see, in Brenda's story, the troublesome effects of children engaging power relations—always a part of human interaction—and how the emotions of human relations enter into intellectual discussion. In one case, we see an example where the power is beautifully balanced, as Kari and Kaitlin seek harmony through their differences. In another, we see a child experience a moment of feeling the power to exclude, and engaging another to assist her. The fact that group work permits more human emotion to enter means it is more enlivened than much direct instruction, yet reminds us there is often more for teachers to cope with. When teachers permit natural conversation, they then face the necessity of being prepared to support children in ways that allow strong participation from everyone: Such preparedness is a necessary component whenever teachers decide to promote group work.

Brenda uses a powerful intellectual strategy. She makes frequent use of an invitation to the children to predict ahead of action. This slowing children down to predict engages their planning capacities. And in concert with predictions, she uses the rereading of transcriptions of sessions as a way of bringing up memory of previous work. Repeated over 35 sessions, these processes of prediction and revisiting allowed a superbly sophisticated retelling of the story of the project by the children in their final child-prepared documentation, something they shared with their families. These iterations, repeated over and over, deepened the connections and memories of the work for the children. Coupled with the children's attachments to each other and to the work, the project became exquisitely memorable to all involved. That kindergarten children wrote pages and pages by hand to describe their research was a testament to their deep commitment and love of the group's project.

CHAPTER 8

The Stretching Starfish
Children's Theories

Noula Berdoussis

In September, as children familiarized themselves with my classroom environment, I realized what a transition it was for them coming from a half-day program in kindergarten to a full-day program in Grade 1. They were so tired and restless by 2:00 o'clock. The rich cultural mosaic of the school was reflected on a smaller scale in the diversity of cultures among the 20 children in my class: Sri Lankan, Pakistani, Chinese, Vietnamese, Jamaican, Trinidadian, Latino. Many students came from lower-middle class families, a few from middle-class families.

My multicultural inner-city public elementary school (pre-K to Grade 5) is in a large urban school system. In this school there are several special education and ESL programs. All children receive a morning recess snack and the school tries to meet the needs of the community: It houses international language programs, an on-site government-subsidized daycare facility, on-site annual dental care for students, and a food bank.

FOUNDATIONS OF EMERGENT CURRICULUM

I was preparing to begin an emergent curriculum—Reggio-inspired—uncertain how it would unfold. As I reflected on fundamental Reggio principles such as the art of listening, the spirit of reciprocity, the voice of visual languages, and the power of documentation, I realized that such principles could not flourish under a production schedule organization of time or within a rigid prescriptive environment. I wondered what would happen if I slowed down and put the children at the center of learning while letting the curriculum silently "wait" in the background? And I wondered, could I, as a public school elementary teacher, work with and interpret Reggio principles within a system that values product over process? As I considered these questions, I also saw potential for exciting possibilities and research—research that would grow from and with the children. Thus I made the decision to give the children playtime for the last hour and 15 minutes of the day. This playtime became my window to listen carefully to the children, to observe play patterns, and to make observational notes. This careful attention to the children's daily play in the early weeks of school allowed me to notice some children's fascination with my personal seashell collection.

The children played "seashell store," keeping inventory of the shells, making lists of customers, and inviting other children to visit their store on two tables. One afternoon I decided to enter the children's imaginary world by visiting their store to "purchase" a beautiful shell to put in my home aquarium. The children welcomed me into their play and after some debate "sold" me the most beautiful shell. I took my shell and placed it in an empty aquarium situated on the window ledge. I believe my play actions inspired what I called "shells in motion" in the following days. Although the seashell store was still open for business, the children's play became more complex as "purchased" shells started to get incorporated into other areas of play, for example in the dinosaur land, in the empty aquarium, with the blocks, and at the drawing table. Later that week, to provoke the children's play further, I filled the empty aquarium with blue-colored water. Although at first uncertain whether they could play with the water, the children quickly embraced the aquarium as part of a new playscape. The shells had a new home!

Sometimes it was difficult as a teacher to deal with the uncertainty of attempting an emergent curriculum. There were times when the volume during play became too loud or when the play appeared short-lived and scattered so that I questioned the value of what was happening in the classroom. Yet despite my uncertainty I had an underlying belief inspired by the Reggio Emilia approach. The daily playtime at the end of the day became the essential ingredient that would lead us toward an emergent curriculum.

Introducing Centers

By late September I decided to introduce activity centers in the classroom. I planned that each center would offer a different "graphic language" of learning. The classroom environment, including five round tables, two rectangular tables in an L shape, and an open carpeted area, made the classroom space flexible and transformable into an art studio. I transformed the space to include centers three to four times a week in the afternoons during the children's designated playtime. The initial centers were sculpting, painting, drawing, and light.

Sculpting. Plasticene was the first sculpting medium. Later I introduced clay. One round table offered five work spaces, each with an acrylic surface, a freshly cut slab of clay, and slip. In the center were sculpting tools like forks, spoons, can openers, and pens.

Painting. At the two tables devoted to painting the children had a selection of fine brushes, various sizes of paper, and a varied color palette with several gradations of blue, some corals, and any other color requests made by the children. When organizing the colors, I was inspired by Reggio educators who believe a varied color palette offers children more creative possibilities (Vecchi, cited in Cadwell, 1997, p. 78).

Using light. At the light center an overhead projector shone onto a giant-sized piece of white paper taped to the chalkboard. The overhead transparencies included images of various sea creatures from our classroom books. Also I included various sizes of paper that the children would tape to the white-paper-covered chalkboard so they could draw their selected magnified image.

Drawing. In the middle of the room, two round tables provided the drawing center. Here the children found various sizes of paper, black felt-tip markers, crayons, colored markers, and pastels.

Classroom library books ornamented these work stations. On the ledge behind the sculpting table I placed books about sea creatures from our classroom library. These books were often used as reference points as the children worked at the sculpting center and at painting and drawing.

Our First Classroom Discussion

When I introduced the activity centers, I held our first classroom discussion around an imaginative question: "If you could truly have one wish, would you want to be a fish" (Ehlert, 1990)? It was through this imaginative channel that Jennifer and Terry expressed their ideas about starfish. I see their initial theories as entry points into our emergent curriculum. Jennifer said, "I want to be a starfish because when you cut them they still move." Terry said, "My cousin says that when you cut the whole body of a starfish that it grows back. A starfish can never die."

Picking up on the children's enthusiasm following the conversation, I invited them to move through the classroom like the sea creatures they wished to be. The children liked the idea, and I soon had angry sharks swimming, friendly dolphins splashing, and then to my surprise Jennifer lay down on the carpet to form a star. Almost half the class joined her on the carpet as they spread their arm and legs and joined hands. "We are starfish!" they exclaimed. I sensed a surge of energy. The children had captured my attention, and I felt I needed to do some homework on starfish.

On that day the sound volume came down to a buzz and the children were fully engaged in their activities. Terry and Jennifer, inspired by the discussion, dramatic play, and color palette, painted an ocean picture. While painting, Terry said to Jennifer, "The class is so excited, it is like a birthday party in here!" So Terry could also sense that something had started.

CHILDREN BEGIN TO THEORIZE

Over the next few days I encouraged the children to share their ideas regarding sea creatures. Prior to each discussion, I had broad guiding questions in mind in order to gently steer the conversation so it remained on topic. Following the discussion, I would invite the children to use the centers to represent their thoughts. One afternoon I asked, "What do you know about sea creatures?" To my surprise and delight the discussion went back to starfish.

Jennifer: I learned that a starfish can grow its leg.
Austin: I think there is another skin and it pushes out.
Terry: Maybe people make starfish … and then the leg grows back.
Diljot: I think the leg just grows by itself.

During this conversation I believe the children started to theorize. When Reggio educators refer to children's theories, I interpret this to mean children's predictions, hypotheses, or ideas that are created in order to explain and give meaning to the world around them. Even when children's theories are rooted in imagination, this is very much accepted as legitimate theorizing by Reggio educators (Vecchi, 2001). The examples of the children's predictions given above are theories because they were created to explain how a starfish's leg could grow back. Reggio educators say that such theories are continuously elaborated, reworked, and thus evolve over the course of a project as children search for clarity; such theories are provisional, not fixed. I hoped that through further discussion, provocation, and graphic representation I could open the possibility for the children to elaborate their theories.

Initial Theories Provoke Retheorizing and Questions

It was quite evident through our conversations that the children were interested in starfish. To cultivate their curiosity, I reminded the class of Terry's theory: "When you cut the whole body of a starfish it grows back." I asked, "*How* do you think the starfish's leg grows back?" Diljot, like many of the children, was intrigued by Terry's theory and was inspired to theorize:

Diljot: When a shark eats a starfish's leg … the starfish's leg will grow back. Something pushes it out like the skin. Maybe it is the bone that comes out.
Austin: Maybe it is the skin that pulls out.
Diljot: The bone pushes out and it grows into a leg.
Austin: They do not have bones, they are jelly. Maybe the skin pulls out.
Diljot: You know starfish. How does a starfish be born? Do starfish lay eggs?

I found Diljot's new theory significant for he built on Austin's theory, "I think there is another skin and it pushes out" to regrow the leg, and he added something new, the notion of a starfish having bones. Diljot and Austin held conflicting theories, for Austin theorized that starfish "do not have bones, they are jelly," while Diljot theorized, "The bone pushed out and it grows into a leg." Equally exciting were Diljot's questions, "How does a starfish be [sic] born?" and "Do starfish lay eggs?" I wondered what I could do with these new questions and how I could provoke the children's thinking further.

Transforming Theories into Questions

An important element in the "pedagogy of listening" is the act of slowing down and relistening to children's conversations. I found that transcribing the conversations immediately after they had occurred was an essential tool in helping me reflect on what the children were thinking. In mid-October I reviewed my transcripts and jotted down the children's questions and reoccurring theories. I felt this review was necessary because I found myself uncertain how to proceed. Once I had my list, I made the decision to take the recurring theories and pose each in the form of a question. I hoped that transforming the theories into questions would open the possibility for further discussion and debate, and I hoped such debate would provoke the children to rethink their theories. I recorded the list of questions on chart paper and posted them the next day in the classroom. These questions became the guiding force in the investigation and, depending on the children and their interests, we would use one of these questions to direct our topic of conversation. I have included the major questions below.

- How do starfish be born? Do starfish lay eggs?
- Do starfish have bones?
- How can a starfish move after it gets cut?
- How do starfish move?
- How can the starfish's body grow back?
- Can a starfish never die?

Diljot's Question as Provocation

I decided to invite a small group of children into a discussion, a group that held a keen interest in Diljot's question. I posed Diljot's question to the group: "How do starfish be born?"

> *Diljot:* Maybe starfish they grow by themselves or God gives them. It [the egg] looks like a ball. Maybe God throws the egg down or maybe another starfish pulls the eggs out, then it cracks. Then what happens [is] it grows another egg, and it grows bigger and bigger and pulls out another eggs so it makes a family.
> *Terry:* When starfish get born they lay eggs and then it cracks and then it grows. And then its mom and dad, it doesn't need them, because they are all grown up and they can take care of themselves. Then they have more eggs. It does it all over again.
> *Shaun:* Me and Diljot found out in this book that the starfish lay eggs.
> *Diljot:* Yes, it comes from the mouth!

The children's fascination and rich theories emerged as they pondered big philosophical questions about the origins of life. Diljot shared two theories, the divine origin of starfish and the starfish's ability to lay eggs, while Terry described the life cycle. Also, Shaun's and Diljot's comment that starfish lay eggs from the "mouth" demonstrated that the children's theories were flexible and thus capable of evolving as new information surfaced.

The second part of the conversation had a surprising shift in focus as the children started to discuss how a starfish's arm grows back:

Shaun: In the book they are actually saying about that red starfish. Actually, the starfish is stretching out its arm. It is pushing out because something eat it. The bones are pushing back out too far.

Noula: Oh. . . . That is what is happening in that picture (referring to the picture of the starfish with the one extra long leg, which the children refer to as the "stretching starfish"). How does that happen?

Diljot: How much it eats is how big it grows. If it eats one bite it grows a little, if eats a lot it will be a big leg.

Terry: When a shark eats a starfish's leg, the more sharks eat its leg the more longer the starfish's leg grows.

Noula: How does that happen?

Terry: I don't know. Maybe it, there is a little bit more parts and then it grows and it gets longer.

Noula: Today when you are drawing maybe you can show me that.

What I found most exciting was Shaun's ability to recall a photograph he had seen in the book *Starfish* (Stefoff, 1997) and to make an inference that the starfish was "stretching … because something eat it. The bones are pushing back out too far." I found Shaun's theory exciting for he had borrowed elements of Diljot's bone theory to speculate that when a starfish's leg gets cut "something pushes the leg out…. Maybe it is the bone that pushes out and grows into a leg." Again I was hearing the theory of starfish having bones. What could this mean?

Conversation as Provocation for Graphic Representations

When small-group conversations occurred, I would invite the members of that group to recap the discussion to the class. This sharing time allowed the children in the class to participate in the reexploration of existing theories, add new theories, and debate existing ones. The generous allowances of time dedicated to children's conversations and the careful listening that occurred acted as the children's provocation to graphic representation at the activity centers.

During this activity time Diljot captured my attention. At the paint center he painted an egg falling from the sky into the sea.

Diljot: Maybe God know[s] we don't have starfish and then he throws an egg and then it grows.

Noula: Wow, that sounds amazing. Can you show me how that happens?

I was so pleased as I looked at Diljot's painting because I recognized that he had combined his two original theories into one representation, the divine creation theory and the starfish having eggs. Shortly after, Diljot called me back. I saw this as a sign that he was really thinking about his theory and as a sign of confidence.

The starfish's egg is blue. It's blue but the white color goes away after. First it [the egg] was white [as it comes from the sky] and then it go in [the water] and the water is blue. And then it becomes the blue egg.

Layer by layer through the medium of paint Diljot was reworking his theory as he searched for clarity regarding his question "How do starfish be born?"

Later that week Diljot's thinking was further captured at the drawing center. He was drawing a starfish that appeared to have a cut arm, and in the distance, a shark. From the cut arm an arrow pointed outward as though something was regrowing. After quietly observing and taking some photos I approached Diljot and asked him to explain. He replied:

> The dots on the starfish are poison and they have to stick. That is the mouth when it is open [points to the center of his starfish]. The shark is dying because he ate the starfish's dots [suckers] and they are poison. The shark ate the starfish's arm and now the bone is pushing out and it grow[s] into a leg again.

As I listened to Diljot's explanation, I realized he borrowed Shaun's speculation that "starfish make poison" to elaborate his own theory, adding that the "dots" (the suckers) were not only poisonous, but required for "sticking." According to Diljot's theory, the starfish was further able to protect itself by its ability to grow back, and for Diljot it was the bone that was responsible for the regrowth of the cutoff arm. This time Diljot had depicted his bone theory. I was impressed for I recognized the cognitive reflection and understanding needed to transfer a theory into a representation.

MAKING CHILDREN'S THEORIES VISIBLE

Pedagogical documentation is a teacher research methodology comprised of two aspects: process and content (Dalhberg, Moss, & Pence, 1999). The content includes the material (or data) generated from the children; for example, the teacher's handwritten notes, photos, snippets of children's theories and questions, the transcripts, and their sample works. Pedagogical documentation as process "involves the use of the content materials as a means to reflect upon the pedagogical work in a rigorous and methodical way" (p. 147). The documentation is reviewed, revisited, and reflected upon as the teacher studies it and asks: What kind of theories do these children have and how can I challenge them? How is it possible to extend the investigation into long-term project work? Documentation as process helps with ongoing teacher planning and also helps shape the emerging curriculum.

Understanding documentation in this way, I wanted to try to make documentation that captured the children's thinking and assisted my planning. I wanted to make children's learning visible, but I was not sure how to arrange the content that I had accumulated. In late September I attempted my first documentation. After looking at the transcripts and the photographs, I decided to feature our first class discussion around the imaginative question, "If you could only have one wish, would you want to be a fish?" I used a poster size bristol board to lay out the story of the day, including the entire transcript, photographs of the dramatic role play, a short segment of the conversation at the paint center, and a brief commentary. When done I wondered, Is this what documentation should look like? Did I make learning visible?

By my fourth attempt I began creating documentation that I felt was more focused. Before I began, I asked myself, What do I want to make visible? After careful review of the content (transcripts, photographs, journal notes), I decided to focus on Diljot's questions: "How do starfish be born?" and "Do starfish have bones?" I felt these questions encompassed many of the children's curiosities. First, I selected an exciting snippet of conversation about his origin of starfish theory and his bone theory. I made sure to include Austin's contrary theory, "Starfish don't have bones, they are jelly." Second, I selected two photos of Diljot's painting of his divine origin of starfish, and third, I included a teacher reflection section where I tried to make meaning of the learning that was unfolding.

Once I had the three parts, I decided to arrange the documentation content into what I refer to as *documentation strips*. This was a new format I was trying out. A documentation strip was one-quarter of a bristol board poster cut horizontally. The strips forced me to really think about what content I absolutely needed in order to highlight the children's theories and shifts in learning. Also, using the strips opened the possibility for me to add future layers of documentation to the existing strips as the project unfolded. With my new strip, titled "Diljot's Theory," I felt what I had in front of me was not a recount of general events in the classroom like my earlier attempts, but rather a captured moment in children's thinking and learning. I used this format throughout the rest of the project as new theories emerged and old theories elaborated.

Documentation as Invitation to Coconstruct Theories

As I thought of the children's theories concerning how the starfish's arm grows back, I recognized the children had embraced Diljot's bone theory with confidence. In thinking about how to provoke the children to consider a different possibility, I decided to use the documentation titled "Diljot's Theory" as a vehicle for provocation. I hypothesized that debate could arise from Austin's theory, recorded in the documentation, that starfish "do not have bones, they are jelly," a theory that was in direct opposition to Diljot's. I invited Austin to a small-group conversation with Shaun and Diljot, for his theory would be controversial because Shaun had not only embraced Diljot's theory but helped elaborate it.

As we sat close to the documentation, I began the discussion:

Noula: Diljot asked two questions that day. He asked "How do starfish get born?" and "Do starfish have bones?" The question I would like to talk about is this. Diljot says that starfish do have bones and Austin says they don't. Shaun, what do you think? Do starfish have bones?

Shaun: Yes, because how can they lift up themselves, they would be too weak. Remember in that book it showed how can they flip. It has to have bones!

Austin (shaking his head No): They don't, maybe the water moves the
     starfish.
Diljot: Austin gave me an idea. Me and Austin's idea. Maybe they got
     bones—only the arms and the legs, nothing else. Maybe the wind
     pushes the water *in* the starfish. It [the water] goes in the middle of
     the starfish and it stays there. The water goes in and the bottom is
     squishy.

The documentation strip acted as a springboard to discussion, and most amazing was the level of listening occurring as the children took each other's theories
and built and reworked their own ideas. Shaun agreed with Diljot's theory while
Austin maintained his adamant conviction and theorized that the water moves the
starfish. The coconstruction of theories was demonstrated when Diljot responded,
"Austin gave me an idea. Me and Austin's idea." Diljot then proceeded to theorize,
incorporating both his own and Austin's theory that "Maybe they got bones, only
the arms and legs, nothing else" and the "middle of the starfish . . . is squishy." I
interpreted *squishy* to mean full of water and boneless. I probed further:

Noula: Okay, so what do you think is inside a starfish? When I look at a
     starfish the arms look so wiggly.
Shaun: You can't see the bones because it has skin.
Diljot: Remember what Jennifer said, that when you cut the starfish it still
     moves and you said, how it do wiggles. Well that is how it moves, it
     wiggles.
Austin: Because it doesn't have bones!

Diljot added another layer to his thinking by drawing upon Jennifer's theory,
which was an entry point into our project work. Austin theory is unchanged, despite Diljot's attempt to draw up Jennifer's ideas. Finally, after much thought and
discussion, Diljot said: "Maybe Austin is right, they don't got bones because it is
skinny. I don't know."
     That evening as I thought about the conversation, I began to see Diljot's ac-
knowledgment that "Maybe Austin is right" as profound, for it demonstrated the
provisional nature of the children's theories. Even though I believe that children's
theories are provisional, until this point I had felt that some of the children were
stuck on the bone theory and kept asking myself: How do I provoke the children to
consider a different possibility? The documentation "Diljot's Theory" successfully
set the stage for debate. This was the first time Diljot considered a different possibility. Also, Diljot's acknowledgment that "Maybe Austin is right" was amazing,
because it got to the core of how documentation can provoke conversation and
thus allow the children to coconstruct knowledge as they search for clarity and
understanding.

Children Document and Theories Shift

I wanted to visit a pet store with live starfish to provide the children with the
opportunity to seek clarification to their investigative questions. We took with us
clipboards, paper, and pencils, and I invited them to record whatever they found

interesting. I too had documenting tools: a camera, my journal, and a tape recorder. At the pet store, I heard excited voices as children saw various wonders of the sea. Most exciting was when the store associate took out the chocolate chip starfish for the children to hold. Shaun at first was quite timid, for he had theorized that the bottom was poison, but as he watched the starfish move on his friend's palm, Shaun worked up the courage to hold it too. The energy was high and after 20 minutes of taking it all in, the children settled down and took the role of documenters. For the next 25 minutes the volume came down as they were completely self-directed and engaged in observational drawing.

After the trip the children's enthusiasm was evident in their overwhelming eagerness to share and discuss their experience. For several days the children shared their pet store drawings and personal experiences, and revisited the photographs I took. One afternoon I held another small-group discussion and asked what these children had learned from our trip:

> *Diljot:* Starfish don't got poison, they got suckers to help them stick.
> *Shaun:* It was scary even [if] it don't got poison, because when the guy put it [in my hand] it [starfish] almost fall. And then the guy said it was going into its shell.
> *Noula:* Going into its shell? What does that mean?
> *Shaun:* That means like he has a shell like a turtle, but I didn't know that, that is something I learned about starfish.
> Jennifer: I am going to try to paint that today (pointing to the picture of the "stretching starfish"). The starfish is stretching out its leg.
> *Noula:* Why is it stretching?
> *Diljot:* I said something. The starfish here when the shark eats the arm, then it grows, the two arms stick together to grow big. The bones grow in.

The children's encounter with starfish had provided them with new factual information and new ideas, such as Diljot's notion of bones growing. Particularly exciting was Shaun's statement that starfish have a shell. This theory was new and it quickly got me thinking about the conflicting theories the children held regarding starfish having bones. I decided it was time to ask the children to stop and rethink.

> *Noula:* Okay let's think for a moment. Do starfish have bones?
> *Diljot:* Yeah, that was my question.
> *Shaun: No!* They don't have bones, they have a shell. They don't got bones.
> Jennifer: I think Shaun is right. The starfish don't even have anything inside. They only have the sticky stuff that comes out. OK, so the shell must be bony.
> *Terry:* Maybe the starfish is the outside with its shell and the inside is the body of the starfish. Maybe the shell protects it.

I saw a shift in thinking as they considered the idea of a shell and slowly moved away from Diljot's bone theory that they previously accepted. Terry complicated matters by making the distinction between the outside of the starfish (the shell) and the inside (the body) while theorizing that "maybe the shell protects it." Vevina, who had remained quiet during the conversation, brought over a classroom book and, pointing to words, read: "Starfish bodies have no bones!" She helped to validate Shaun's theory and I wondered whether the group was ready to accept the new information.

> *Terry:* Oh, starfish have no bones!
> *Diljot:* Yeah, Shaun, you were right. Starfish have no bones!

Diljot, through the collaborative effort, had gathered enough information to accept and validate Shaun's theory. In doing so, Diljot was abandoning his own bone theory for he found clarity and understanding in another idea. This was a major shift for Diljot!

The final part of the conversation took a different path, for I was able to choose work samples to add further complexity to the discussion. By children's work, I mean their graphic representations that were displayed in the classroom. I brought to the circle Diljot's drawing depicting how the bone makes the starfish's arm regrow. Once Diljot reexplained his bone theory, I posed to the group a very challenging question:

> *Noula:* You guys just now told me that the starfish doesn't have bones.
>   Tell me now how you think the arm would grow back then?
> *Shaun:* There is jelly.
> *Diljot:* If the starfish gets cut and didn't have bones, then how did it grow
>   back?
> *Terry:* It stretches out.
> *Diljot:* But, how does it stretch out?

From a moment of certainty—"Yeah Shaun, you were right. Starfish have no bones!"—came another moment of uncertainty. Diljot's framework of thinking was being challenged. We can really get a sense of Diljot's thinking as he restates the question. His friends are actively engaged and willing to help create new theories by drawing on their understanding of the "stretching starfish." Diljot is not yet clear as he asks, "But, how does it stretch out?" After listening to Shaun's and Terry's ideas about a starfish being jelly and stretchy, Diljot reshapes his theory:

> *Diljot:* I think when it gets cut off, the skin is jelly and when it stretch the
>   jelly goes in and maybe inside it is sticking and sticking.
> *Terry:* Remember when I said I was watching this show and this guy cut
>   a starfish and its arm just grew back. And the other arm that was cut
>   grew another starfish.
> *Noula:* What? One arm became a new starfish! Do you think that is
>   true? Can you maybe draw a picture to show me how that happens
>   because that is incredible?

Terry's idea was the beginning of something big: I realized the connection between his new theory and the "stretching starfish," and I wondered if the children, with time, would see it too. Would Terry be able to represent this theory and how would Terry's new theory help the children in their understanding of how starfish regenerate? I grew excited just thinking about it!

Graphic Representation Clarifies Theories

I created new documentation strips highlighting the discoveries made from our trip to the pet store. I highlighted Shaun's contribution that starfish have a shell and Terry's theory that the cutoff arm grows into another starfish. I thought it was important for the small group to meet again and to focus on Terry's new theory.

> *Terry:* People might cut the starfish and then it grows more starfish. If you cut an arm or a leg it grows from that. It is so interesting! If you cut the whole starfish into pieces it will grow so much.
> *Noula:* So you are telling me if a starfish has five arms and all five get cut off then each arm will grow into a starfish?
> *Terry:* Yes, and the starfish with all the cut arms will stretch out. A starfish can never die, because it always can grow back. It can't ever waste a leg.

At this moment Vevina, a quiet listener, got up from the circle and went to the white board. She said she would draw Terry's idea. As we watched, I was not sure what she would do (see Figure 8.1).

In her diagram Vevina depicted two starfish. The first is an adult starfish with a cutoff arm. The adult's cutoff arm had a baby starfish regrowing from it. Here was the "stretching starfish" in a new light. I believe it was Terry's ability to further develop his theory that helped Vevina find clarity in her understanding regarding what happens to a starfish's cutoff arm. Terry's theory was represented visually, and I knew the children were slowly getting closer to understanding Diljot's original question: "How do starfish be born?"

In the week following our conversation the children's theories were richly represented through various "graphic languages" of learning. As I observed the children, I sensed a surge of energy. Diljot was at the drawing center working on a book about starfish. Here he represented his theory on how starfish are born (Figure 8.1): "The egg comes outside and when it cracks a baby starfish comes out." He used the arrow to show how the baby starfish comes out of the egg. He then explained, "The baby starfish can come from the cut arm too." Diljot's theory was a composition of coconstructed knowledge combined in a rich, complex, and scientific way as he tried to represent the dual reproductive nature of starfish. I could not help but smile as I thought of his first theory, "Maybe God knows we don't have starfish and then he throws an egg down." My chest swelled with pride—I could not believe how far we had come!

Exciting things were unfolding at the clay center as the children continued to represent their theories. Valeska, a quiet student, rarely verbalized her theories

FIGURE 8.1. On the left, we see Vevina's "How a starfish grows": She shows a new starfish regenerating from the cut ray. On the right, Diljot's theory of how starfish are "born"— from eggs or from a cut ray.

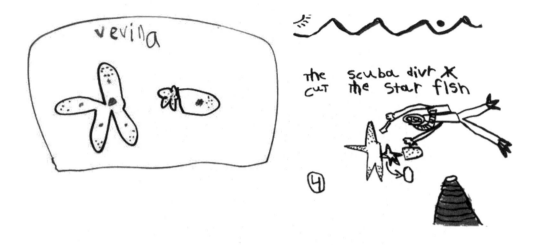

during discussions but thoughtfully expressed them through graphic representations. Valeska told me, "I am going to make a starfish and how it is going to get born." How was she going to do this using clay? She started by using the clay to make a detailed starfish. Then she made seaweed and added an egg. She created a baby starfish near the egg as though it was emerging from it (Figure 8.2).

I saw the children's representations as gateways into their thinking, allowing me to follow the evolution of their theories over the course of the project. As their theories became clearer, so did the children's representations, and their understanding deepened through their use of graphic languages. It was amazing that shell store in playtime had led us to a biological exploration of the reproductive abilities of starfish.

TEACHER REFLECTIONS

During this project I challenged my conventional definition of *teaching*: To teach did not mean to transmit knowledge, but rather to enter a new relationship with children, one based on reciprocity. According to my new definition of *teacher*, I needed to become a careful observer and listener, to provide generous and flexible allowances of time, and to provoke children's thinking through higher level questions that encouraged critical thinking and inference-making. I also needed to layer content in the classroom environment to support thinking. These layers included the centers, classroom library, documentation strips, and the children's graphic representations. It was this redefined role of teacher that encouraged the children to emerge as empowered researchers in an emergent curriculum, one that was coconstructed.

This journey with emergent curriculum was full of uncertainty. At first, dealing with the uncertainty was difficult, for I felt as a teacher I should know what to

Figure 8.2. Valeska's "birth of a starfish" in clay.

do next. I believe this feeling of "I should know" comes from working with standardized curriculum (Ministry of Education and Training, 1998c) and the sense of comfort it creates for teachers in knowing where they are going as they follow a prescribed list of expectations within preset timelines. But as the project progressed, I learned to embrace uncertainty, for it made me stop, reflect, and question what was happening in the classroom and how I could better support the children. Being able to stop and reflect slowly brought clarity regarding the next steps and the possible direction of the emerging curriculum. Most important, the uncertainty allowed for the unexpected, the surprises.

It was as much a learning experience for me as for the children, for together we shared discoveries, challenges, and conflicts. We carved our path slowly, not knowing for certain where we were heading, but always moving forward with momentum, and finally arriving at a place we never could have imagined.

CAROL ANNE'S COMMENTS

Noula is a teacher who understands how moving among several complex processes of teaching builds connections in children that propel learning further. She consciously layers many different ways of learning—using adult reference books; using graphic materials such as paint, clay, and light; supporting children's conversations; generating careful documentation; revisiting documentation. I think she uses these teaching processes almost like aspects of a dialogue, in which use of one layer affects use of the next. This capacity to work consciously with multiple frames of reference for viewing children's knowledge generation and to layer them—thinking about what should come next to open up thinking, feeling, and learning—is a sophisticated capability found in the most creative teachers. Other contributors in this book also do this, but this way of consciously layering multiple rich processes for learning is laid out particularly well for the reader in the final three chapters.

Plate 1. *First Painting of Lightning.*

Shows orderly, brown-yellow lightning bolts.

Plate 2. *Second Painting of Lightning.*

This painting of lightning at sunset shows growing understanding of the complexity of lightning's shape and colors.

Plate 3. *Third Painting of Lightning.*
Sapphire's painting of lightning in daytime shows bolts coming down fast and sporadically.

CHAPTER 9

"I Am Your Lightning Girl"
Building Relationships with Inquiry

Diana Will

There is a crispness to the beginning of a school year—the sharp pencils, eager faces, and a wealth of promises given and not yet broken. I was excited to be back in the classroom after several years of support roles, and to start inquiry with my Grade 2 students. I knew there would be challenges ahead as I tried to carve out time for an emergent curriculum approach within the constraints of the standardized curriculum. I believed that I could use the children's interests and progress to find connections within the given curriculum to provide the interactive, relevant, complex, and concrete activities that Bredekamp and Copple (1997) define as part of emergent curriculum.

I started by setting aside an inquiry time of 1½ to 2 hours twice weekly during my morning literacy block. This was a time for students to interpret their experiences by proposing, planning, engaging, and sharing individual and group projects that evolved from questions they had about topics of their choice. *Inquiry*, "the act or instance of seeking truth, information or knowledge about something" (Martinello, 1998, p. 164), would be a frame for the curriculum. Inquiry would place a value on meaning construction through the shared questions, observations, problem solving, and spontaneous discovery of the students and myself.

INQUIRY BEGINNINGS

I believe inquiry is embedded in wonder so I wanted to create an environment where there were many opportunities to discover and wonder. I was not sure how to begin "observing with a wondering eye" (Whittin & Whittin, 1996, p. 88). How do you create a classroom that values wondering? I thought my own wondering was where to start. Through September we wondered together as a class: How did we get our names, what things could change, and how were we changing as a class? We interviewed each other and our families, drew pictures, explored nature, and discussed what we noticed about our interests. I remember reading a book on creative writing that gave the advice to make the familiar seem strange, so that we look at it again in a different light (Wilson, 1983). I guess my intent in those early school year days could best be described as trying to make the familiar strange.

111

While excited with what we were doing, I must admit to some early disappointment. What seemed most strange to me were my students. When we engaged in community-building activities, it felt more like policing-prevention exercises where I was diffusing potential conflicts and separating students instead of bringing them together peacefully. When we engaged in conversations, it was my voice that filled the spaces between one-word answers. When we engaged in sharing our wonderings, I wondered how I was going to sustain attention past 5 minutes. I was overwhelmed by the academic, emotional, and behavioral needs in my class. This was the first class in my career that would put me in the running for our school's "cup of endurance" award—a not-so-coveted honor. How would my very practical, very needy children embrace inquiry?

I wanted to avoid what Audet and Jordan (2005) call "sham inquiry," which focuses on what teachers find salient. So I embraced the notion behind emergent curriculum that is illustrated so beautifully by Reggio Emilia's long-term inquiry projects—following the children, not the plans (Malaguzzi, 1998). As my class led me to inquiries about animals, my thinking table took on an animal flair with bird feathers, animal photographs, and other animal-related objects. The animals that the students inquired about seemed to change day by day as they bounced from question to question.

By December, I realized I had just assumed students would use their interests to generate interesting questions that would then lead them to inquiry projects. The students' goals appeared to differ from mine, as their goal became one of asking as many questions as possible and to show quick answers to the questions. I wondered whether my students really knew why they were asking questions during inquiry. I was reminded of Dewey's (1933) point that people learn when they seek answers that matter to them. I wondered how much the answers to their questions mattered to my students.

How do I teach why we inquire? Unsure, I began to approach teaching questioning in three ways: directly talking with the students about why I ask questions, listing the questions they had and analyzing them, and modeling my own questions and wonderings with the inquiry groups. From September to December, we were exploring what it meant to ask "real," "effective" questions. The students had to step out of their ways of thinking, "scripts" that they relied on, for studying their world. I began to see the role of inquiry as one that allowed students to shift away from a problem-solver mind set to a problem-poser state of thinking. "Real" questions are elusive and harder to ask, for sometimes there are no known answers, or many theories. "Real" questions require students to embrace uncertainty, and they lead to more questions.

By February, most of my students were beginning to inquire. They were starting to play with their interests—drawing, dramatizing, building, and so forth—in ways I had not seen previously. Their questions became less generic and were more focused on the aspects of animals and nature that were real to them (e.g., "What happens to broken hippo teeth?" and "How do penguins use their bellies to slide on ice?"). Over the year, sustained inquiry projects encompassed approximately twenty different topics, including how a volcano erupts, what ancient sharks were like, and why lions sleep a lot. Most topics were about natural phenomena and were explored in a multidisciplinary manner using scientific, artistic, linguistic, and other ways of knowing. I went from feeling like I was digging deep to find evidence of my students' imaginative ideas to feeling like I was racing to keep up with them.

Yet more than halfway through the school year there was still a dark cloud on my inquiry horizon: One of my students was not an inquirer. Sapphire did not perceive herself as an inquirer, and, moreover, did not like inquiry time. I felt like I had two insurmountable forces to bring together—inquiry time (and all my confusions around what it was and could be) and Sapphire's attitude towards it. This chapter illustrates the journey Sapphire and I took as she taught me about the more divergent paths to inquiry of some students. She made me question what it means to inquire and how we create a culture of inquiry in the classroom. How can we help students like Sapphire build a relationship with inquiry, a relationship that encompasses oneself, other people, and the domains of knowledge and affect that their imagination seeks?

I teach in a midsized, urban school identified by its board of education as high in its "learning opportunity index," which is based on economic and social-cultural data: average income, single-parent families, number of single detached houses, education levels within the community, number of students who arrived in Canada in the past five years, recent immigrants in the school's neighborhood, and student mobility. The school is in a low-income area with many high-rise buildings. My classroom contained 21 six- and seven-year-olds with significantly more boys than girls (15 to 6). About one third to one half of my students received some form of special education support. About half spoke a language other than English at home—primarily Spanish, Vietnamese, Cantonese, or Farsi. Also, about half were of Caribbean descent.

Sapphire was 7 years old and turned 8 during the course of the year. She lives with her mother, half sisters, half brother, and her niece in a family of six members. She is Black and of Caribbean heritage. According to her Grade 1 and 2 report cards, Sapphire was struggling with some literacy and mathematic areas.

I audiotaped and transcribed our discussions and took photographs of children and their work; these were displayed in the classroom and used in my master's thesis (Will, 2007). I kept a reflection journal on the inquiry process and notes from that journal are combined with transcribed conversations in this chapter to reveal my thoughts.

Wandering Through Inquiry

In the fall Sapphire wandered through inquiry time. On good days she would join a group sketching, then move to a group building with tools, and then look at a couple of books. It was the students who were participating in the activities that drove her choices. By January, she was one of only two wanderers left. Inquiry time was not the only time that Sapphire experienced frustration; however, it was a challenging time that was affecting her relationship with learning, the class, and myself. Sapphire would react emotionally and defensively to any provocation. Her days were filled with regular peer conflicts where she either hit or yelled at other students. She had considerable difficulty taking responsibility for actions that even I saw her take and then had difficulty handling the consequences. Yet Sapphire could also be very caring toward younger students and displayed a great deal of love to her family and slowly toward me as her teacher. She enjoyed arts and social studies activities, but struggled with literacy and math. She would sometimes "shut down" or withdraw from activities by choosing to take a "time out." Often she needed to be coaxed into learning situations.

In December, I started Sapphire on a behavior tracking record (a weekly chart with goals and comments) that chunked her day into blocks with set goals and the possibility of earning stickers and other rewards. Her aggressive behaviors began to lessen. Yet she still expressed frustration when faced with tasks requiring more open-ended or challenging responses, such as inquiry time. For example, one inquiry period Sapphire chose to sit by herself, doodle on a piece of paper, and then rip it aggressively to shreds.

By the winter term, inquiry had become a standard feature of my classroom and a huge vehicle for learning. If a student could not engage in it in the same way as other students, I wondered how this might affect that student's learning. I felt that Sapphire wanted to be successful at inquiry but had no idea where to start. It was easy to see that Sapphire was just not engaged in any activity or project for longer than a half hour. It was harder to determine what led to this lack of engagement. I thought perhaps her wandering was a sign that she was unsure—unsure of what she was interested in, unsure of her abilities, unsure of what it meant to be engaged with learning, unsure if she could be successful.

I watched for moments of success within the inquiry period where Sapphire appeared more engaged. I recalled the fall day when she came to school excited about her new shoes and, with prompting, spent a whole period sketching her shoes using a magnifying glass. Her drawing was surprisingly detailed (see Figure 9.1) and she said she liked to draw. I thought perhaps drawing could be her entry point to observing the world and communicating what she noticed. While I suggested arts activities and provided interesting objects to notice, Sapphire accepted the invitations I offered about a third of the time. I noticed she would be more likely to engage in sketching if one of her friends was sketching beside her. Often though, this arrangement led to more disagreements rather than a supportive learning context.

I must admit that my attention was being pulled in so many directions during inquiry time that sometimes it was easier to let Sapphire wander or do anything as long as the class was not disturbed. I felt as if I was laboring, with inconsistent results, to figure out what my intentions were as a teacher for inquiry time. Why was it important that everyone engage in inquiry time? Was that a realistic expectation? My energy was sapped by the knowledge that there was so much potential in inquiry time and yet there were students who could not engage in it.

In December Sapphire explored our Dr. Seuss book bin and read for 20- to 30-minute periods. In January she brought her own Dr. Seuss books from home to put in her inquiry bin. I sat with her several times to read a Dr. Seuss book, and wondered aloud about the author and his ideas. I put paper and a fancy pencil in Sapphire's bin and said she could draw or write about the books. She began to

FIGURE 9.1. Sapphire's sketch of the sole of her new shoe, her first use of inquiry time to explore something closely.

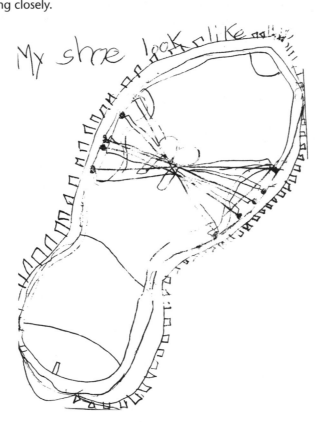

My shoe look like...

copy painstakingly the words in the book. I wasn't really sure where this activity was heading, but I was glad that Sapphire had found something to do during inquiry time.

Looking back at the points where Sapphire had, and had not, made contact with what it means to inquire, I noticed that Sapphire was engaged with stories, drama, and visual art, but did not appear to know how or where to begin applying that interest to an inquiry topic. She did ask some questions about her world ("Why does my sister's baby need 9 months to grow inside her?"), but did not really work with different "texts" in the classroom as resources. Yet as Sapphire's reading and writing skills improved, her confidence in her ability to communicate and her engagement with tasks improved. She seemed uninterested in working with the boys in our class, and that left only five other students with whom to interact. She appeared interested in the everyday things around her—her family, her friends, her clothing, and her environment. She was not interested in the animals, bridges, or shells that other inquiry groups were pursuing.

I wondered if Sapphire required more guidance and if by assuming inquiry would just happen, I was missing the opportunity to help it happen for some students. In February I gave Sapphire a choice of children to work with (she chose two girls in the class) and I engineered an opportunity for them to explore weather books in a guided situation with me. Most of this conversation focused on the tsunamis, hurricanes and storms in the news, and on the resulting destruction and death. It seemed a kind of morbid fascination, a secret subversive interest in things powerful and uncontrollable—and reminded me a little of Sapphire who sometimes felt like a powerful and uncontrollable force in our class.

After several occasions of reading pictures in the weather books, the girls raised the question, "Where does rain come from?" It seemed like the kind of question they thought they should ask, rather than originating from their interests, yet it led to Sapphire's first "I think" explanation in her inquiry book:

> I think rain comes from the air in the sky and from water. And when
> the rain comes donw [sic] It makes big puddles and I like to jump in the
> puddles and the rain has little drip and thir [sic] is air in the sky and
> when it feels like the sky is full of water so it pours out a lot of rain.

This writing was lengthy for Sapphire and connected to personal experience. She was excited about what she wrote, her friends were excited about what they all wrote, and her teacher was excited. Sapphire had experienced her first successful foray into wondering and questioning during inquiry time.

The "I Wonder" from the Sky

Sapphire was talking with her coinquirers about lightning and its power to destroy. From that talk came this written response from Sapphire in late February:

> Sometimes when it rains the thunder and lightning comes from the sky
> and when it is tomorrow some times it gets foggy outside and also when
> rain comes it get foggy too and some times it scares people.

I wrote underneath Sapphire's writing, "I wonder," challenging her to think of something she wondered about storms. I gave her an example, "I wonder how lightning comes to the ground?" I expected to come back and see a similar wondering. I was surprised to read, "I wonder if the storm has color?" This wondering was unexpected, apparently simple and yet so complex that it could be explored in many ways. Excited, I told her I loved her "wondering" because it made me picture in my mind all the different colors a storm could possibly have. Surprised, she looked at it again and said, "Really?" Later that day I heard her proudly tell other students that she had found a great "I wonder," as if the "I wonder" had fallen from the sky as a gift.

For a week, however, it appeared as if this gift was put aside. I assumed Sapphire had lost interest, but she surprised me again when she revisited her question about the color of storms and connected it to her interest in lightning in early March, by asking, "I wonder if lightning has a color?" She attempted to answer her question in her inquiry book: "I think it as [sic] a yellow color because some time I see in the book and it is yellow." I wrote back, "Is it all yellow? How or why does it get yellow?" No response. So I engaged in this conversation with her:

> *Diana:* Now you are wondering if lightning has a color. (pause) That would be kind of neat to see. What do you think you need to do next to figure that out?
>
> *Sapphire:* To look in a book.
>
> *Diana:* So we need some books about lightning? And some pictures of lightning? You know there are pictures that are like photographs, which are real pictures. But there are also pictures that are paintings of things that artists paint that are their ideas of what lightning is. Should we look at both maybe?
>
> *Sapphire:* Yes.
>
> *Diana:* Okay.

I felt like I was struggling for words along with Sapphire. Tentatively I asked— or was it more of a direction?—"Now, did you want to start with your picture of what lightning looks like to go with those words?" I felt like Sapphire had a great question but did not know what to do with it. I also felt like I was doing most of the talking and making the choices for her. How could she engage more fully with her topic?

A BRIDGE OF ATTACHMENT TO THE QUESTION

I wondered if I was talking with Sapphire about the right things—her ideas—or if talk was the mode of expression she even needed. I also wondered how much my passionate response to her color of storms question had helped her connect to the topic of lightning and storms. What role did I have as a teacher in helping students build a relationship with inquiry? There is an assumption that inquiry begins by having children focus on their interests. Sapphire taught me the important role that other influences, such as peers and teachers, can have in hooking students to topics. Sapphire's friends encouraged her to consider lightning in the first place, and my reaction prompted her to revisit a question about lightning's color. Maybe Sapphire's disengagement in inquiry required someone else's engagement with her ideas to help build a bridge of attachment between her and her topic? Rinaldi (2003) points out that to deeply understand "involves the ability to experience curiosity, passions, joys and angers of others with a process of empathy, perception and identification of human understanding" (p. 4). I had to reinterpret my teaching choices to discover ways to experience curiosity and emotion alongside my students. This reinterpretation felt strangely hopeful.

Freedom and Choice

Sapphire established a predictable inquiry routine for herself during March and April. She was engaged in trying to capture lightning with her sketches. Dur-

FIGURE 9.2. Pencil sketch of lightning.

ing one sketching period I asked her about the shape of lightning, which led to about eight pencil sketches that focused on lightning's shape, not its color (see Figure 9.2). It was interesting that she chose drawing, with which she had previous success, as a means to know lightning. I also noticed how my comments influenced her representations.

There was an interesting mix of independence and uncertainty in Sapphire's inquiry. During three inquiry periods she chose to turn a desk so that it faced the wall and work silently on her sketches. It was an interesting nonverbal "stay away" signal. I asked her once how her drawings were going and she responded tersely, "Good." Yet her hunched body posture did not reflect this same confidence. I didn't want to limit her imagination by what she thought she could and could not do well, yet her "leave me alone" attitude made it hard to read the uncertainties beneath or to find ways to approach her.

Yet I felt the uncertainties were there. One day, she threw several of her sketches in the recycling bin. Another day, she asked me if it was okay to spend her time drawing: I sensed doubt about how to use her inquiry time and even what it means to inquire. I asked her jokingly if she was sketching bananas. Puzzled, she replied, "No, lightning." After asking why she was sketching lightning ("to see it") and what she was learning ("Lightning is not straight and it is very hard to draw") and what kind of resources she was using to help her ("The lightning book and I watched the lightning video and lightning outside once"), I hoped Sapphire was starting to understand that her drawing was a way of learning about lightning.

I feel that to become passionately engaged in learning, children have to feel free to choose where to invest their curiosity, intelligence, and emotions. When young children are not used to making choices, I suspect the teacher needs to make explicit the potential in their choices and the successful outcomes that result from them.

Ideas and Intentions About Lightning

After 3 weeks of drawing, Sapphire chose to paint lightning. Her first painting revisited her earlier understanding of lightning as reflected in her drawings with lightning bolts orderly and evenly spaced (see Plate 1). The color of her lightning strokes, however, showed a golden glow around a solid brown center. Lightning was not just "yellow" for her. Her second painting (see Plate 2) showed lightning "like the sun and the sun is just going down. And it is going darker." For her third painting (see Plate 3), Sapphire was "trying to get the shape of lightning from this picture here but make it daytime lightning," using a photograph for inspiration. I began to sense Sapphire's developing theories about lightning through the artistic choices she made:

> *Sapphire:* The clouds are stormy and are spread across the sky—like in books—you see them flat. The lightning—the lightning comes down from the clouds—but—the lightning—you can't see it because it is so fast and the clouds are spread out. You look at the lightning and not the clouds.
> *Diana:* So how are you going to paint the lightning?
> *Sapphire:* I'm gonna paint—use this thick yellow paint and have it come down like this one—all over—down, down, down—so it looks quick.

By early May, Sapphire represented lightning as coming from different directions, thick, fast, and occurring at different times of the day. There was also scientific understanding that lightning could occur in low-level clouds with flat, dark bottoms like cumulus clouds. Moreover, Sapphire was actually talking about lightning in an authentic way, in contrast to our earlier stilted talk.

Sapphire's paintings, contrasting "sunset" and "daytime" lightning, showed the ideas she was working out about how the time of day affects the color of lightning:

> Morning lightning is just a kind of, kind of a blackish color. And if it is night, you can see really lightning—kind of a yellowish color. Because

night can make lightning show and when it is morning, lightning cannot show.

She explained, "Lightning just changes itself. We see it in different ways or colors," hinting at her knowledge that lightning's color is not determined by us, that what changes is how we perceive lighting at different times of the day. The act of interpretation requires, based on observation, a perception of reality and a perception of what is not there—the implied and the possible. Sapphire later linked lightning's loud sounds with its brightness causally. Sapphire's imagination appeared to help her see and hear lightning in a creative way.

Before drawing and painting lightning, Sapphire perceived its colors in a more restricted way. In fact, one piece of writing in March suggested she *feels she knows* what color lightning can and cannot be:

> It is always yellow because it cannot be pink red and sometimes it can be black and yellow. How does lightning look it looks like it has point sids [sic] that is strong. Sometimes I can hear lightning when I am at home inside my room.

After engaging in representing lightning through paintings and drawings for over a month, Sapphire noted more possibilities for the colors of lightning:

> Sometimes lightning can be red or sometimes lightning can be red but it is really yellow. People think it is red. . . . Maybe it change different colors. Sometimes—because the last time when I saw lightning, I saw kind of a goldish color.

How did Sapphire's inquiry choices influence the development of her theories?

Artistic Choices and "Repicturing" Lightning

Sapphire's disengagement with inquiry dissipated not only when she established an attachment to her topic, but also as her method of inquiry, the arts, required cognitive, physical, and emotional engagement. The arts demand engagement: you pick up the pencil and you mix the paint and these experiences pull you inside what you are creating as both participant and audience to that creation (Booth & Hachiya, 2004). It is interesting to speculate how Sapphire's perception of lightning changed when she chose to imagine it in an artistic, visual and emotional way. For example, the act of choosing to capture lightning through painting resulted in a need to consider other visual qualities of lightning such as its shape. Her drawings and paintings reflected a change in how she perceived lightning from falling straight down the page in evenly spaced columns (see Plate 1) to having an overlapping energy with twisting, crowded shapes (see Plate 3).

I wanted Sapphire's confidence in her ability to inquire through art to grow. I tried to provide a balance of honoring her approximations of lightning and providing feedback. By reacting emotionally to her work, I hoped that I could keep my feedback real so as to support Sapphire's continued engagement in her "fun" project and yet offer provocation to her learning. In May I asked her if she could use another medium to show the colors of lightning, hoping to expand not only her "literacy in art" but also her connections to lightning in a way that would build confidence and her understanding of lightning. Sapphire chose chalk. Her chalk picture's background moves from warm colors to a cooler blue and, while her lightning is not all linear in shape, it has a downward direction. I noticed some red lightning strokes, a choice Sapphire said she made "because lightning. . . it kind of be light and red." Not only do her paintings now reflect her words that "lightning can be different colors," they also show connections to previous understandings ("This one is also daytime lightning") and new techniques with chalk ("They were turning different colors and I took my hand and started spreading them around"). Sapphire's artistic choices here showed a growing enthusiasm and confidence.

In June Sapphire said, "Lightning can be many different colors." She elaborated on that idea, with prompting, describing lightning as "sometimes yellow but really goldish. It can be a little red or pinkish. At night it looks more gold but can be a little purple or—or very light blue. Sometimes, sometimes lightning is so light that it is white."

The development of her ideas about the color of lightning from always yellow to the range of colors she lists in June is astonishing. But while there were many results from her inquiry, it is Sapphire's growth in confidence that she can inquire in her own way that I celebrate the most because that confidence will propel her to learn more in a future that extends far beyond Grade 2.

Becoming Lightning to Know Lightning

In June Sapphire further expanded her theories about lightning and her ways of knowing. Focusing on lightning's colors, shapes and effects led to questions and ideas about the hows and whys of lightning. When I asked Sapphire, "I wonder why we have lightning, if it is hurtful?" this fragment of conversation occurred:

Sapphire: We have lightning because of the clouds and storms.
Diana: Do you know how lightning is caused?
Sapphire: It is electricity inside the clouds when two clouds hit each other. In the movie, they talked about how some people believe that God causes it or that he is angry.
Diana: What do you think?
Sapphire: I don't know. God may have made the clouds but the clouds may make the lightning.
Diana: I wonder why people always think of lightning as someone being angry. [I am caught up in genuine questions now, not just for the sake of modeling, but also for the sake of my own discovery.]
Sapphire: Maybe because it is loud and can look angry. It can have angry shapes.
Diana: What kind of angry shapes?
Sapphire: Shapes that are very—pointy—got points—like zigzags.

Sapphire showed her imaginative, metaphorical thinking in which lightning is viewed as having "angry shapes." I cannot help but engage in my own metaphorical thinking when I view Sapphire's lightning inquiry as a creative outlet for the "angry shapes" inside her. Theories now lead easily to new wonderings, as when Sapphire voiced the thought that "maybe different shapes of clouds. . . give different shapes of lightning."

In mid-June Sapphire was ready to try new ways of exploring lightning. When I offered her the provocation to "pretend that we are lightning in a cloud," she agreed. She put restrictions on the activity (like a metaphorical desk facing a wall) such as she was "not going to face the lion group," but would be "facing the chalkboard." Yet the class's comfort with different inquiry displays was such that they let this dramatic play unfold unchecked. Sapphire began to embody lightning by springing up, arms in rigid, twisted shapes.

> *Diana:* Tell me what you are doing,
> *Sapphire:* I am bouncing like lightning.
> *Diana:* I am also going to bounce in a nearby cloud because I think lightning sparks off each other. [I begin to bounce farther away from Sapphire.]
> *Sapphire:* Lightning bounces in clouds together and then has to poke through the cloud and—and flash down. It makes zigzag shapes and can become two lightnings.
> [We bounce a bit more, sometimes close together and sometimes far apart.]
> *Diana:* How does it become two lightnings?
> *Sapphire:* One half goes like this one way—the other half goes like this another way.
> *Diana:* You called it little squirly things that go from one lightning to another.
> *Sapphire:* Yeah they go like this. . . . [Sapphire travels across the carpet in a twisting shape.]
> *Diana:* Sapphire, why do you think lightning twists?
> *Sapphire:* It twists because it thinks—decides—where to go—where to hit.
> *Diana:* How does it decide?
> *Sapphire:* It sees what is on the ground and sometimes has time to go and sometimes it just flashes.
> *Diana:* Why does it just flash?
> *Sapphire:* It is going—going so fast—and maybe there is—is so much rain.
> *Diana:* So it doesn't have time to decide where to go?

Sapphire doesn't answer my question. Perhaps it was getting too hard to answer questions and bounce simultaneously. I also think my questions unintentionally break up the rhythm of our enactment. Sapphire stopped bouncing and then asked her own question.

Sapphire: Ms. Will, why does lightning hit some things and not—and not
    other things?
Diana: What do you mean?
Sapphire: Why does lightning hit one house and not another house?

In the process of transforming her thinking, Sapphire was also transformed through arts inquiry from a disengaged, frustrated learner into an active learner with the freedom to display her curiosity about lightning by spontaneously asking questions. She imaginatively gave lightning humanlike perception and thought processes—lightning can "see what is on the ground" and "decide" where to hit. Lightning has become anthropomorphized, suggesting a more personal connection to it. The power of drama to isolate, capture, and simulate increasingly abstract and complex concepts such as the direction of lightning is clear. Her embodiment of lightning showed her developing ideas that lightning flashes, splits, and is unpredictable in shape and force.

I can see in Sapphire's vision of lightning her ways of knowing about her world. Her reflection on what makes one lightning stroke different from another also shows what makes lightning the same:

Diana: What makes lightning different?
Sapphire: It's shape and color. Sometimes it is at night and sometimes—
    sometimes it is in the day. It will hit some things and not others.
    Sometimes—sometimes it hurts people and sometimes—sometimes
    no one is hurt. Some people—they are afraid of lightning—and some
    people think lightning is beautiful. But lightning just is. It is just
    different in many ways—like cultures and people are different in
    many ways.
Diana: Wow. That is such a neat comparison—to think about how
    lightning and people's cultures are the same and different. That is
    some powerful thinking there.

Sapphire's response strikes me as extremely philosophical: Lightning and life changes, everyone perceives it differently but tries to understand it. By seeking out lightning's differences and similarities, we try to understand what lightning is all about—but lightning just is. It's how we understand it that influences what lightning is to us. This comparison between people, cultures, and lightning overwhelmed me with its power, eloquence, and deep thinking.

The fact that the eloquence and deep thinking here was not evident at the beginning of Sapphire's inquiry did not surprise me. The fact that she required time to immerse herself in the topic and to allow a multitude of expressive ways to develop is affirming of inquiry methods, yet not surprising. What truly surprised me was how much the act of inquiry was an act of thinking about what it means to be in the world—to be in the world as a teacher, as a human in relationship with others. Sapphire saw in lightning immense beauty and destructiveness, but also the people of her community and the world she imagined outside of what she knew. Inquiry enabled this discovery of the world for one child.

TEACHER REFLECTIONS

Inquiry is a relationship builder. Any relationship is about connection. Sapphire's inquiry began when she discovered that someone was interested in her "I wonder" about the color of storms. She became excited about lightning when others were excited. Her engagement with inquiry rested on the bridge of attachment being formed between her, others, and her topic. It is humbling to note the role the teacher's desire, search for context, and persistence plays in enabling emotional bridges of attachment. Inquiry is about developing this connectedness of teacher and student actions that grow out of and are rooted in our shared beliefs in children as creative, thoughtful and resourceful. My love of her question about the color of storms became a bridge she could traverse to love lightning in her own way.

Once the attachment to the inquiry topic was established, I believe the act of making choices to portray lightning visually and experiencing success with those choices were crucial elements in Sapphire's developing relationship with inquiry. Feeling successful at one mode of expression fueled Sapphire's further engagements with other modes of expression such as drama. As her inquiry opened up, so too did her theories about lightning and her understanding of her ability to inquire—the power within herself to learn.

The act of making choices through continual playing with different roles (scientist, artist, performer, theorist, writer, audience member, critic) and experiencing success were crucial elements in Sapphire's developing relationship to inquiry. Each role shift (i.e., from painter to dramatist) allowed Sapphire to try a different viewpoint, with its particular methods, tools and approaches for learning and expressing knowledge, enabling her to build a questioning relationship with her topic, to deepen her understanding of lightning, and develop her confidence in her ability to inquire. This process of trying out texts, roles, and, ultimately, knowledge is a way we let our imagination play through a topic.

I cannot help but wonder what kind of imaginative thoughts my students might have expressed if they were used to a more developmentally appropriate emergent curriculum in their schooling. What if an inquiry curriculum were taught without the subject-time specifications? Or if curriculum was viewed as the connections among the big questions of subjects and students' interests? An inquiry curriculum that supports imagination uses information not to answer, but to question and imagine the "always more" that exists in our world.

On the last day of school Sapphire said to me, "You will remember Grade 2 and me, Ms. Will, because I am your lightning girl." This insistence that I would remember her seemed strange at first, because how could I forget Sapphire? But then I thought how the power of this claim lies in its demonstration of Sapphire's personal identification with her topic. That Sapphire was a "lightning girl," by her own admission, seemed profound because she was like lightning in my mind: changing, volatile, forceful, powerful, and beautiful.

Sapphire's inquiry recalls the challenge that Gallas (1994, 1995, 2003) repeatedly identifies for teachers: to ensure that the range of experiences in our classrooms is broad enough to reveal each child's voice so that we can know them and to ensure that those experiences spring from events that the children have shared together. Sapphire's feeling of powerlessness at the beginning of inquiry time merely highlights the power of inquiry and different methods of knowing and representing such as the arts to transcend limitations placed on children by language or life experiences. Sapphire's imaginative life is beautiful and that life needs an expressive connection with the life of school. The Sapphires of this world need to be pulled into the life of the classroom or they risk being marginalized. Sapphire taught me to have faith in the complexity that teaching requires, faith that as a teacher I can navigate the unscripted life of learning and believe, know, and convince others that children can and do learn through inquiry.

CAROL ANNE'S COMMENTS

I love the way the data that Diana presents during their in-role bouncing, pretending to be lightning, shows how this activity, and her teacher's participation in it, supported Sapphire in generating a new question. She suddenly wondered what determines where lightning strikes. We see how new inquiry spins out of embodied in-role enactment. It is a compelling example of the generation of thought in a child.

Overall, is there any greater gift a teacher can give a family than to draw into serious relationship with learning a child who has difficulty finding herself in school? Diana assists her in finding her own relation to powerful learning, helps her develop visual languages of learning, and finds the child opening to wide thoughts that show a mature stance toward the world.

CHAPTER 10

"Can Weaving Make a Horse?"
Kang as Protagonist

Mary Jane Miller

In January an interest in weaving was sparked by a 9-year-old Grade 3 student in my class. He arrived with a thin wooden board wrapped with light blue yarn and announced that he would teach anyone who was interested to weave. There were 27 Grades 3 and 4 children in our urban public elementary classroom. The children were primarily from working-class homes with a small number of professional or middle-class families. Many of the children spoke English as a second language. At home they spoke Cantonese, Vietnamese, Mandarin, or Portuguese. Very quickly a network of weavers grew. Children were weaving on little cardboard looms during recess and activity time; and by the end of February, everyone in the class was weaving during story read-aloud. The children also enjoyed several opportunities to weave on a giant chicken wire loom I set up in the classroom.

Weaving on the large-scale loom and their own smaller looms generated much discussion so I invited the children to write down their questions, ideas, and theories about weaving. After studying this writing, I focused on six children whose projects I documented closely: Amy, Jia Ling, Adam, and Polly, who were 8-years-old; and Kang and Matthew, who were 9. These six children represented a diversity of linguistic, socioeconomic, cultural, and academic backgrounds.

To signify the active role that children take in their own research, I use the term *protagonist*, as do the educators of Reggio Emilia (Cadwell, 1997, 2003; Filippini, 1998; Rubizzi, 2001). Five of the protagonists' initial questions related to shapes, designs, or ways to weave (e.g., "Can I weave a triangle?" or "Can I weave a zigzag?"). In February Kang's question, "Can weaving make a horse?" caught my eye as I was reading through the children's writer's notebooks. I was intrigued and wondered what Kang could possibly be imagining. Here's how Kang introduced his question to his peers:

> *Jia Ling:* What do you mean by weaving a horse? Do you mean weaving a square first and then weave a horse on it, or just weave a horse?
> *Kang:* Like just weave a horse—like kind of a real horse, but it's kind of different. You can make the tail with leftovers.
> *Amy:* I think you can't really weave a horse but you can make a horse

> with all the weaving shapes you done. Like you weave a square can
> be the head and maybe one part of the weaving can be the horse's hair.
> *Kang:* Like some of the good weavers can make a different kind of things,
> like the harder things that people can't make, and the easy ones.

Some may regard Kang's question as absurd. However, I wanted to legitimize his idea by setting up a listening context with his peers. To take the time to carefully listen to children's questions, ideas and theories is to value children's perspectives (Dahlberg et al., 1999; Rinaldi, 2003). During the conversation, Kang didn't respond to my invitation to illustrate his ideas so I met with him several other times to find out more about his ideas. He told me he would like to weave a horse that he could play with. He motioned with his hands to show that he would like the head and legs to twist and turn and the tail to move. I asked Kang again if he would like to draw his ideas. He responded, "I don't know how to draw a horse, I think." He offered to try, and drew three ovals and three tails: "And here's the tail and beside it, there's another tail right over there, then another tail."

During this exploratory stage, I felt like a detective, taking seriously every detail of Kang's amorphous ideas. My impression was that he imagined new ideas as I posed questions even though my intention was to understand what he was thinking and not to steer him in any particular direction. I tried very hard to understand and follow his line of thought. It was a kind of attentive listening that requires being mindful of the present while simultaneously recording what he is saying and doing.

When I understood that Kang imagined three horses, I wanted to know more about his plans for one horse. "So help me understand. If this was one horse, then how would you make the one horse?"

KANG'S FIRST DESIGN

Once Kang had a number of opportunities to play with his ideas, I asked him many questions, nudging him each step along the way into making his ideas clearer and more specific, both by talking about them and putting them on paper. I invited him to draw more details so that when he shared his ideas with his classmates, they would understand how he planned to go about weaving the horse. I also believe that drawing and writing about his ideas encouraged Kang to plan and consider more deeply the details that would be involved in making a woven horse. Our discussion began with Kang explaining that the oval he has drawn is the body, a fat body.

> *Mary Jane:* What would you be making it fat with?
> *Kang:* With … you know—the weaving string.
> *Mary Jane:* So show me how you'd do that. What have you drawn here?
> *Kang:* It's the body. It's the fat body. . . . You can just go like down and
> then you can just go up, down, until you've covered the whole place.
> *Mary Jane:* What will the weaving look like?

Kang: Like kind of fat and stuff.

Mary Jane: How are you going to do that?

Kang: You can just cut out a cardboard. Then you can just use string to wrap around it and you can just make a fat body.

Mary Jane: So draw the picture here of the cardboard. What would the shape of the cardboard look like?

Kang: A circle. . . . Actually a fat one like this kind.

Mary Jane: Yes. Sort of like an oval. So that would be your cardboard.

Kang: Then you can make strings all around it like this.

Mary Jane: How are you going to get the strings around like that? The yarn like that?

Kang: No, like, you started from here. Then you just have to weave.

Mary Jane: So actually draw what each piece of yarn would look like. So where would you start?

Kang: Here.

Mary Jane: And it would wrap around behind? Okay.

Kang: And then keep on going until it's all covered up.

As I found myself adjusting my questions according to Kang's responses, I was reminded of Malaguzzi's metaphor of a Ping-Pong game to describe the two-way interaction between me and Kang: "For the game to continue, the skills of the adult and child need appropriate adjustments that allow the growth through learning of the skills of the child" (Malaguzzi, 1998, p. 68). I wondered if one of the reasons behind Kang's reluctance to draw was that he doubted his abilities. With this hypothesis in mind, I tried to provide him with varying degrees of support: first by pointing out where to draw the body, then by getting him to consider its shape, next by providing him with the name of the shape, next by getting him to consider and draw where the yarn would start and finally, where it will wrap around. Kang's intentions were becoming clearer, but I still had many questions. What was his notion of a "real horse"? What was his perception of "fat"? What image did he have in mind: two-dimensional or three-dimensional?

After such questions and explanations about the projected weaving, Kang drew his first horse, illustrating how the yarn would be wrapped around the body. He suggested: "I think it will look like a real horse. A flat one. It would be like a giant book and you squashed the horse. Then it can be flat."

I suggested Kang share his design with a small group of peers. The children's questions and comments encouraged Kang to be clear about his ideas and to think further. Even though Kang's voice was barely audible, his five classmates sat quietly as he explained his design. To Kang's credit, he patiently repeated his explanation four times. After the first, I asked him to speak so that everyone could hear him. After the second, I asked the children if they could hear him. No. After his third explanation, I asked Jia Ling if she understood what Kang meant. She asked Kang to repeat what he has just said!

Kang: It's like this is the horse. This is the cardboard, right? You just have to cut out the horse head and then you cut out the body. Then you cut a tail. Then you can put some glue on it. And then you can stick it altogether. Then you can stick it all together and then you can just weave on it.

Adam: How would you weave on it?

Kang: You just have to make a kind of—do a horse—like weaving it so—

Adam: So you weave around this part?

Kang: Yeah. You can weave around that part. You can weave the body.

Karen: How did the body parts go together?

Kang: You can put glue on it. Then you can stick it together.

Amy: I don't think that pieces of weaving can stick together but they could only go together by sewing it.

Adam: No. I think he means glue the cardboard together.

Mary Jane: How could you tell whether that's what he means?

Adam: Kang, do you mean gluing the cardboard together?

Kang: Yeah.

Adam: Or the yarn?

Kang: Cardboard. Glue the cardboard together.

The discussion process was painstaking, as I wanted to ensure that everyone understood. I don't like to be as involved as I felt was necessary during this conversation because it slows the process and interrupts the rhythm, but I believed it was the time to set the stage for meaningful exchanges. I wanted to get across to the children that the active participation of each and every one of them is valued. I wanted the children to realize that making oneself understood and understanding one another is what is important in these discussions.

Making the Loom

As Kang finished drawing the horse on the cardboard, he commented, "It kind of looks like a dinosaur." It did look like a dinosaur with its thick, forward-stretched neck and small oval-shaped head. I noted Kang's frank observation, and, because of its significance, included it with the photo of his loom on the documentation posted on the chalkboard.

With Kang's horse-shaped loom cut out and waiting to be woven, I had many questions about its design, its future, and my role. Should I help Kang improve on the design of his loom so that he would be pleased with the results? Do I intervene, or is it more important that Kang continue uninterrupted with his exploration? The cutout horse pieces look quite small. How would he be able to glue the pieces together? Could he weave around such tiny legs? Kang did seem satisfied with his first horse-shaped loom. How did Kang feel about his own capabilities as a weaver? How would my decision influence the way Kang felt about himself and his project? Would he become discouraged? I revisited my reflective notes and recalled something he wrote in his notebook: "Is weaving hard? Is weaving good or bad? Is weaving fun?" At that time, Kang shared with me that he had tried weaving, but it was too hard. He added: "Some people think weaving is bad because they can't do it and they do it wrong." These words provided me with Kang's perspective about weaving and, perhaps, the way he felt about his own abilities.

After considering all the possibilities and reviewing the documentation, I decided to watch Kang glue the cardboard parts together and see what happened. The potential problems that lay ahead, given the loom's precarious construction, might lead to challenges and opportunities for learning that would be far more valuable than my intervening at this point. As Kang waited for the recently glued pieces to dry, I asked him to look over his plan. What did he think about his loom? "Yeah, it's good." His body posture didn't reflect the same confidence, so I decided to probe further. During one of his conversations with the small group, he had said, "Like some of the good weavers can make a different kind of things, like the harder things that people can't make, and the easy ones." I didn't want Kang to limit his imagination by what he thought he could and could not do. Instead, I wanted Kang to imagine possibilities, so I asked him, "If you were the most creative weaver in the world, what would you want your horse to look like?" Kang responded "The legs would be taller. The head would be medium shape and the tail would be short." I waited to see if his response would prompt Kang to modify the loom he has made. It did not.

Weaving the Horse

As Kang wove the horse loom, he took it upon himself to resolve each of the problems he encountered: He reglued the body after it separated from the head and three of the legs fell off. When he was done, I considered in my reflective notes the inherent graphic, technical, and conceptual challenges he had faced, his responses, and future possibilities (see Figure 10.1):

> What now? I'm not sure that anyone would recognize that Kang has made a horse. As he said himself when he was drawing on the cardboard, "It looks like a dinosaur." I'm thinking of having him present his horse to the group, but I don't want them to discourage him. Will he be discouraged and not want to try another one? Maybe I need to ask him, "If you were going to do another horse, what would you do differently?" Or should it be, "If you were going to do this over again, what would you do differently? What do you like and what are you happy about?" Perhaps I'll meet with him at the beginning of music period tomorrow and ask him when or if he would like to show the class his horse. I think I need to help him make a horse that is recognizable. Find some pictures of horses and go back to his initial drawings.

Reflections on Kang's First Horse

To help me reflect more, I turned to Kang. I suggested that he read the documentation displayed on the chalkboard. It featured some of his own designs, significant words and photos illustrating conversations with the small group about the possibility of weaving a horse, and how to go about it, as well as photos and words related to the process of making the loom. By reviewing the documentation, Kang could also reflect on his thoughts and actions. Once Kang reviewed the documentation, I asked him what he thought about his horse. He shared these thoughts:

Figure 10.1. Kang's first woven horse.

I like about it, I like the body; the body like big. And the tail, I like about it because I made it. Just like my Mom says: if I make something, right, she says it's—she *loves* it.

By paying close attention to Kang's responses through the documentation and through discussion, I learned more about his feelings, interpretations, and thoughts. They also guided me toward future directions. Based on Kang's response that he liked the size of the body and the tail because he made it, I decided we needed to go further. As Kang's teacher, I believed that he was capable of advancing his thinking further and that I could play a part in making this happen.

We spent time reflecting on each body part he liked and why. I wanted him to consider more things that could be improved beyond length of legs and size of head:

> *Mary Jane:* If you were going to do this horse over—and I'm not
> suggesting you are because it sounds to me like there are parts that
> you are pleased with—but if you were going to do the horse over,
> what would you do differently?
> *Kang:* The head.
> *Mary Jane:* And what do you mean? Tell me more about that.
> *Kang:* The head kinda looks straight. Horses can't keep on looking
> straight all the time.

With more explanations and with Kang motioning with his own head and neck, plus a drawing, I understood that Kang meant he would like the neck to be slanted upwards in a diagonal direction instead of the way it juts out in a horizontal position.

I then invited the small group to read the documentation and have a discussion with Kang to revisit what he had done, the difficulties he encountered, the strategies he had used, and the issues that were still unresolved. The children zoomed in on Kang's notion of a "real" horse:

> *Adam:* What do you mean by a real body?
> *Kang:* Like kind of a real horse body with the weaving.
> *Adam:* How can you make a real horse?
> *Kang:* No, not a real—no, I mean, not a real one.
> *Adam:* Well, what do you mean by real then?
> *Kang:* Like you could—you can make it, kind, like, you could just *look* like a real, a real body.
> *Amy:* Do you mean like as weaving the outside and then stuffing the horse?
> *Kang:* (pause) Well, like it looks like a real horse.
> *Adam:* But what would you do to it to make it look like that?
> *Polly:* Would you have to give it a heart and organs and stuff?
> *Kang:* No. Like one, like, like you can make the head kind of look like [a horse].

During the conversation, I was watching the dynamics, paying attention to the children's level of involvement, and asking many questions in my mind. How was Kang feeling? Were the children sensitive to the difficulties Kang has in expressing his ideas? Does their insistence that he explain what he means so that they understand illustrate that they believe that he is capable of doing so? Or is it making him feel inadequate? Was the encounter too harsh and were there other ways I could support Kang to explain what he means? At the same time, I believe that Kang is highly capable and doesn't need to be protected. My concerns were offset by the engaging conversation that took place, one I saw as a precious opportunity to advance the children's ways of thinking.

Throughout this conversation, I found myself thinking about when to intervene to keep the conversation on track and when to stay back to see how it unfolded. This tension reminds me of Rinaldi's (1998) comment that the "challenge for the teacher is to be present without being intrusive, in order to best sustain cognitive and social dynamics while they are in progress" (p. 118). In this instance, I noticed that by taking time to wait and therefore encourage the natural development of the dialogue, I was rewarded by the children raising the same questions that I had in mind.

Other equally impressive details about this conversation included the children's high level of engagement and the underlying seriousness and importance of the discussion. How did this happen? First, I think that the documentation triggered the children's memories and precipitated the topic toward an important detail. Second, the children really wanted to understand what Kang meant by a "real horse." Along with this genuine motivation, the move away from conversations that focus on who is right, who is wrong, or who knows more, toward a focus of understanding one another shifts the hierarchy. I think that the combination of a significant topic, genuine motivation, and focus on understanding encouraged more children to participate. I also think that because I stayed on the sidelines, each child participated more actively than if I had been more involved. My being outside of the circle for most of the discussion pressed the children to realize that the onus was on them to understand and to make themselves understood. I believe that it also pressed the children to think much more deeply. They had to consider others' perspectives, and perhaps change or modify their thoughts and words. Peers questioning peers can be very powerful as they see how clear and convincing their thoughts need to be.

The children sensed I was keenly interested in the conversation because I took photographs throughout and also tape-recorded it. I think of Piaget's and Reggio educators' shared view that conflict can play an important role in prompting children to restructure their thinking (Rankin, 1997). One possibility was that Kang saw firsthand that the words he used were not making clear what he meant by "like a real horse."

A "Real" Horse

To find out whether, according to Kang, a "real" horse has to be three-dimensional, I suggested he flip through the book *What's the Most Beautiful Thing You Know About Horses?* (Van Camp, 2003), featuring George Littlechild's colorful, childlike painted illustrations of horses. When Kang pointed out to me and the small group several illustrations that looked real and several that didn't, I was still not completely clear about his notion of a "real" horse. The children, on the other hand, were satisfied with his explanations. They were more interested in Kang's plans for his next design so I took their cue and invited Kang to draw a horse.

KANG'S NEXT WOVEN HORSE

Kang drew a wonderfully expressive horse with long legs. I was tempted to use this drawing for the design of his next loom but I decided there was potential for further exploration and research (see Figure 10.2). When I asked if he thought his younger reading buddy would recognize that he had drawn a horse, he was not sure. I pointed out a horse needs ears and hooves. Kang wanted to know what hooves were, so this became the opportunity to bring out books with many photographs of horses to show him. We talked about what we noticed, describing various body parts. Eventually, I suggested Kang choose a photo of a horse that he would like to draw. Kang's second drawing was completed on the same day, the result of close observation, discussion, and reference to the photo. Kang seemed pleased with his drawing and I was delighted. The thinness of the body and legs still needed to be addressed, but I decided we could return to these details later.

Group Ideas for Kang

When Kang shared his drawings with the small group, the most wonderful discussion happened. The children were intrigued by his two drawings and asked him questions about the techniques he used to draw various parts. Amy suggested Kang bring over the books and show them some of the photos to explain some of

Figure 10.2. Kang's expressive horse with long legs.

the details in the legs he had drawn. The discussion took unexpected twists and turns. Amy asked: "Kang, for your next one, are you going to weave the whole body or just here to over here?" More questions emerged: how would he make the head and legs? Would he cut out separate body parts or an entire horse? Would he weave the head and legs too? Would he make the horse bigger than his previous one? Because of the high level of engagement, I decided it was an opportune time to point out that Kang originally wanted a horse whose neck and legs could move. I asked Kang if he was going to ask the small group for suggestions on how he might do that and he agreed. Amy had an idea, catapulting the discussion to an even more intense level, "Maybe you could use some pipe cleaners and put the pipe cleaners inside the horse." When Kang asked, "Amy, what's a pipe cleaner?" they patiently described it and offered suggestions about how pipe cleaners could be used. The discussion was fast paced as the children generated questions and ideas. Even after a break for recess and choir, the conversation continued with the same fervor and interest. This was an arduous process as the children tried hard to make clear their ideas for how to make the horse's neck and legs move. It required repeating, clarifying, considering other viewpoints, building on one another's ideas, demonstrating with materials close at hand, and discussing the merits and problems of their designs. The children were intensely engaged. Finally Amy said, "Maybe we could write down our ideas of how Kang should do it, and then we could meet again and then show our ideas." It was a marvelous suggestion, well received by the group, and embraced wholeheartedly by me.

I reveled in the realization that the children were carrying on the conversation themselves with only one interjection from me to nudge Kang to consider with his peers how to make the appendages movable. What distinguished the later conversations from the early ones was the growth in communicative skills and exchange of ideas. I watched in amazement the energetic focus and quick pace at which ideas were generated, discussed, and questioned. What a contrast to some earlier discussions where my involvement was needed to sustain interest and try to ensure understanding. Perhaps those earlier interventions helped set the groundwork for the children to exchange ideas in this sophisticated way. It was inspiring to see the children take on the role of provocateurs as they asked Kang questions. Malaguzzi (1995) and Gambetti (2004) talk about respecting the rhythms of the children. In this episode, respecting the children's timing and processes and having confidence in their many competencies resulted in the children advancing to richer, further evolved thinking and design work. As for me, I reaped the rewards of listening, waiting, and welcoming what uncertainty can bring: wonderful surprises that exceed what I had imagined would take shape within one day.

By placing value on the interactions among children, I think this encounter highlights Vygotsky's (1978) belief that social experiences play a crucial role in shaping ways of thinking and interpreting the world. Amy's suggestion of using pipe cleaners opened up the discussion to the generation of new and exciting ideas that added further richness and complexity to everyone's thinking processes. I reflect on how the discussion began with Kang showing his drawings and the significant role that this documentation played in launching the knowledge-building process. I also think of Rinaldi's (2001) assertion that "learning is the emergence of that which was not there before" (p. 43).

Amy, Jia Ling, Karen, Adam, and Polly took the initiative to put their theories for how Kang's horse could move on paper. Their designs were clear and detailed and reflected the astonishing degree of thought and consideration that went into them. Amy's design coincided with her theory of creating a stuffed animal by sewing together two woven bodies, filling them with cotton balls and using pipe cleaners for the "horse bones" and the legs. Jia Ling and Karen, who worked together, illustrated an elaborate use of pipe cleaners to create the horse's skeletal system. Adam illustrated step-by-step how to insert the pipe cleaner into the interior of corrugated cardboard and included a superb side-view diagram illustrating this procedure (see Figure 10.3). Polly's design showed the pipe cleaners used for the legs and neck and taped to the cardboard body. Except for the mane and tail, the entire horse would be woven.

I was impressed by the wide array of inventive, valuable, and possible ideas and intrigued by their development. The process of transferring ideas onto paper required Amy, Jia Ling, Karen, Adam, and Polly to revisit their ideas, select which

FIGURE 10.3. Adam's plan of how to make the legs and head of Kang's horse move.

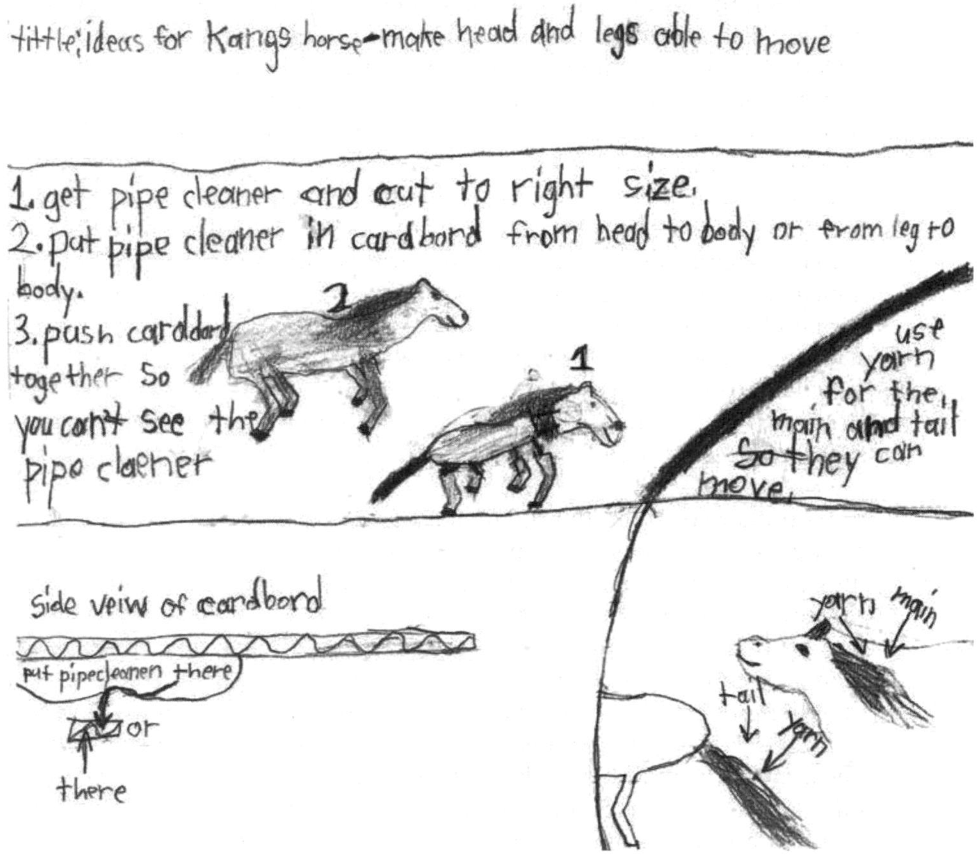

tittle;ideas for Kangs horse—make head and legs able to move

1. get pipe cleaner and cut to right size.
2. put pipe cleaner in cardbord from head to body or from leg to body.
3. push carddord together So you can't see the pipe claener

use yarn for the main and tail So they can move.

Side veiw of cardbord

put pipecleaner there

or

there

yarn main

tail main

ones they would represent, and decide how. I am convinced that these experiences and many others with peers and their teacher to listen, discuss, document, reflect, modify, and invent ideas, all play a significant part in the construction and coconstruction of knowledge.

I was also encouraged by how serious the children were in their work. Very little intervention was needed on my part to ensure their designs were clear, perhaps because in this situation the shared objective grew out of a real problem and the suggestion was generated by one of the children. The motivating force may have been the children's genuine desire to make their written explanations and diagrams understandable to Kang and one another. They knew they would be using their designs for discussion and further work. As Malaguzzi (1998) states, graphic expression is a "tool of communication" (p. 92) that helps children see firsthand the need to be clear and understood.

Kang met with the small group twice, and Amy, Jia Ling, Karen, John, and Polly showed their designs and explained their ideas. For 4 weeks Kang read over the designs repeatedly, talked to me about them, and consulted his peers to clarify details. As the children's ideas began to sink in, he became very engaged and focused.

When the children met to share their designs, I was struck by their patience and persistence to ensure that they were understood. One of the conversations lasted 50 minutes. Kang listened more actively and was more engaged. What could explain Kang's more active involvement? Could it be our insistence that he explain in his own words what each of his peers was saying to show he understood? Could it be the underlying assumption that Kang is capable of understanding his peers' designs? I thought that it was a combination of these and many other influences, such as the emphasis on meaning making and the inclusion of the children in advancing this process; the use of the children's designs as a basis for serious, purposeful discussion; the use of props to help the children explain their intentions; the willingness of the children to try language and questioning techniques suggested by me to engage Kang in the exchange. There was also a social-emotional aspect related to Kang's perception of his competencies. Each time Kang explained his understanding of the children's designs and saw that it coincided with their meaning, his awareness of this growing understanding boosted his confidence.

Another consideration is the temporal dimension to Kang's increasing level of engagement. During the first conversation in which ideas about how to make movable appendages were first being introduced, I recall wondering whether the exchange was a bit beyond Kang's reach. In Vygotsky's (1978) well-known zone of proximal development, I think of the teacher's responsibility to watch out for when the child is ready to take the necessary jump toward learning. Some educators might question why I would have the children endure such lengthy conversations and spend so much time trying to make sure that everyone is understanding one another. Why not just take Kang aside and explain the designs to him myself? I think that such an approach assumes that children learn in a linear, lockstep way and that knowledge can simply be transmitted. From the first conversation about movable legs and a neck to the creation of Kang's own design, it is my interpretation that bit by bit Kang considers new ideas, reflects on them in relation to his own understandings, and adjusts his thinking accordingly. It is my observation that this constant restructuring of understanding takes place in a back-and-forth, circuitous way. With each new learning situation, from discussing the possibilities, to viewing the designs, to meeting with his peers in a group and individually, Kang's growth in learning (and for that matter, all participants' learning, mine included) didn't happen in a linear way. I would argue that it is through revisiting his peers' ideas in a variety of contexts that Kang's learning has grown. The Reggio principle of circularity (Malaguzzi, 1998) is now clearer to me, as is its significance for their interpretation of Vygotsky's theory. According to Rinaldi, children learn from many rich problem-solving situations that encourage them to revisit and rerepresent their thinking, either on a moment-to-moment, day-to-day, or week-to-week cycle (as cited in Edwards, 1998). This circular way of thinking and proceeding means that each time Kang revisits these ideas, he deepens his understanding.

Kang's Second Design

Kang decided he would use ideas from everyone's designs to create his own. He was reluctant to draw how he planned to use the pipe cleaner and cardboard pieces but agreed with Polly's suggestion to write down his ideas. Beginning the design was a struggle for Kang. I know all too well how the challenge of deciding what to say, how to say it, and how to organize it can seem overwhelming. Despite Kang's hesitancy, I thought he was ready and just needed some support in starting; he had a number of solid ideas about his next design. Just as reviewing the documentation supports me, I reviewed my notes with Kang that included his ideas for his next horse. My asking Kang "Two cardboard pieces, or one, for the body?" set him on his way. Something very exciting then happened: Kang drew small visual aides at the top of his plan. He had developed his own system of symbols to transfer his thoughts to paper! At this moment his writing and engagement accelerated. A tiny oval labeled b represented the body, and t for tail. The remaining two (L for legs; H for head) were noted just before he wrote about each of them. The d stood for done. Kang's writing plan was clear and organized. It was a great beginning.

It was inspiring to see that Kang needed much less support to write his plan, than he did 2½ months before. I was impressed by how he reread his design, made corrections, and checked spellings. Perhaps Kang realized his design had a number of real purposes. First, as a tool of communication, his design needed to be clear and understandable so that it would help him share his ideas. Second, it would be his reference for creating another woven horse.

Nevertheless, when Kang read his design plan to me, I wondered where exactly he planned to place the pipe cleaner. His drawings served as a basis for a lengthy discussion; eventually, I understood that Kang had invented his own use for the pipe cleaner. In Kang's completed designs, he incorporated some of his friends' ideas, some old ideas from his first woven horse, and some new ones. Despite Kang's initial reluctance to draw, I was impressed by how his whole demeanor seemed much more relaxed and confident than when he made his first drawings. He sang and chanted as he drew: "And the heady! You made the neck too shorty!" It was exciting to see his progress and how he now noticed and made adjustments to his design.

The Second Loom

All that was needed before making the loom was a final horse drawing. Kang chose his observational drawing and traced the satisfactory parts. He redrew pointy ears and made the body thicker and shorter. The front legs went through several changes. He first drew the hooves backwards because he was referring to a photo of a horse facing the opposite direction to his drawing. He found another facing the same way and redrew the hooves. He then redrew the front legs yet again, this time making them smoother. Kang pointed out that pronounced bumps would make it hard to cut out of the cardboard. I was pleased that Kang was thinking ahead, impressed that his intense concentration had paid off.

We enlarged the completed drawing on the photocopier to a size we thought would work well. Kang glued the cutout paper body parts from his enlarged drawing directly onto cardboard for his loom. The cardboard was stiff: He cut out some pieces and accepted help from a classroom volunteer and me. All but the hind legs of the loom were ready. Would Kang notice that the hind leg was shorter than the front leg? I placed a piece of paper where the ground would be and he could see the front legs touched ground but the hind legs were too short.

We studied the hind leg, noticing its shape; he said it was "curved like a C." Actually, the whole hind leg looked like a backward C. Kang and I went back and forth offering increasingly accurate observations about the hind leg, using the horse photo and other props as visual support. After many drawings, the final leg Kang drew was gorgeous (see Figure 10.4).

This episode was especially exciting because it highlighted the processes and potentials of learning for both of us. From my perspective, to watch for opportunities to advance Kang's thinking, to notice his readiness to make the jump, to act upon these observations, and to witness the learning that takes place was very rewarding. By loaning Kang the observation that the hock is at the halfway point of the leg, he paid back this loan of knowledge even more than I expected: He drew a dotted line. It was an ingenious idea.

As Kang worked on his loom, I noticed changes in his demeanor. Matthew casually walked by, stopped and watched Kang and commented, "Oh! That's a good horse." As Kang attached the pipe cleaner to the hind leg, he responded to his own rhetorical question, "Is this good? Yes!" and excitedly rubbed his hands together. As he admired the four legs that were now secured to the body, he smiled and clapped happily. Kang and the horse were coming alive.

Perhaps Kang was experiencing the pleasure derived from all his many efforts at learning. Perhaps he was seeing his own competencies grow and was aware that his classmates were noticing too. Kang spent most of the day voluntarily working on his loom. Energy increased and so too did Kang's confidence in his abilities. He decided to make modifications to the design of the tail that I think were a marked improvement. A poignant moment that I can still picture is seeing Kang, near the end of that day, beaming with excitement and pride as he brought over one of his friends to see his horse.

Weaving the Horse

Weaving the loom presented many challenges because of its irregular shape. One of the most significant episodes occurred when Kang began to weave. He decided to *warp*—wrap the yarn around—the entire horse head very loosely. This resulted in a messy overlapping of some strands of yarn. What a pivotal moment! It highlighted my own uncertainty about how to proceed. There was the actual weaving to consider. Would Kang's approach lead to a satisfactory result reflective of what he had worked so hard to accomplish? Could we improve the weaving? Would, for example, adding slits to the cardboard prevent the warps from overlapping each other? I did not know and did not have expertise in weaving. I felt overwhelmed by the dwindling number of school days and exhausted from the late

FIGURE 10.4. Loom for Kang's second horse.

nights working on the documentation panels. I wondered if I should intervene. How would my questions influence Kang? Would he become frustrated? Give up? Should Kang continue without reflecting more? In the end, I decided that I could not give in to low expectations at this crucial point when the way he began to warp and weave the horse would influence the rest. Reggio educators talk about keeping everything in connection, and I suppose this is what I inadvertently did.

With Kang's first woven horse and a patch of his flat rectangular weaving in front of us, I pointed out he hadn't added slits to his first horse: How could he make the texture of his second horse's weaving look as even as his rectangular weaving? Kang's explanation revealed he had carefully considered the reason why his first horse became so difficult to weave: He believed that he had warped it too tightly, thus his care to warp his current loom loosely. Neither Kang nor I were certain about how to proceed. Kang readily accepted my suggestion that we ask Jia Ling, who had had much experience weaving circles. But Kang sank into his chair and became quite tentative when explaining the problem to Jia Ling. At that moment, I felt my greatest fears had been realized, that my suggestion had ruined everything. I wondered if, by doubting myself, my suggestion caused Kang to doubt his own abilities.

Soon, however, ideas were bounced around, and Kang's self-consciousness dissolved. He became actively involved once he realized he was to make the deci-

Figure 10.5. Jia Ling and Kang weaving.

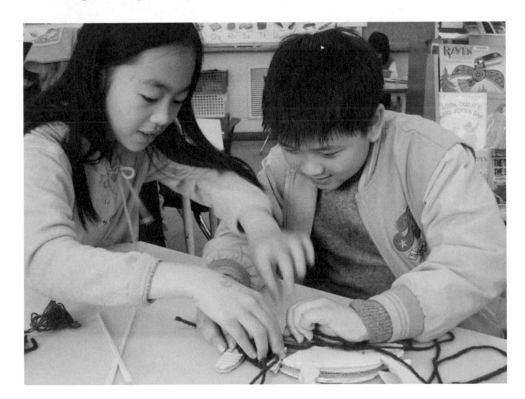

FIGURE 10.6. Kang admires his horse.

sions. Kang and Jia Ling decided to weave the neck first and then the head. It was as if the recent positive experiences propelled Kang toward a deeper connection with his work. He chose to spend full days weaving, except for brief 15-minute breaks for lunch and time out for gym. Jia Ling offered her expertise at tying the final strands and weaving the trickier parts. The collaboration worked well, as they took turns alternating rows and pointed out to one another when they missed something. They worked together for long stretches of time in deep concentration. Interspersed were moments of playfulness and delight (see Figure 10.5).

When completed, Kang's horse did indeed stand up, and its head and legs were movable. It was beautiful (see Figure 10.6). While the completion of Kang's horse is a source of great joy for Kang, his friends, and me, it represents far more than the pursuit of a finished product to answer the question "Can weaving make a horse?" I think it is an expression of determination, growth, friendship, collaboration, laughter, and joy. I also think of it as a metaphor for the wonderful process of building complex systems of relationships among children, teachers, and parents toward a deepening understanding of one another and the world around us.

CAROL ANNE'S COMMENTS

When Mary Jane shares with others the full documentation of this emergent curriculum project with Kang and his classmates, we can see the story of his growing confidence and competence visible in the liveliness and differentiation in how he uses his hands, and in his facial expressions: His face alters from a sort of blank puzzlement to joyful animation and self-respect. We see his teacher taking his whimsical question seriously and the extraordinary capabilities that children show when supported by sensitive teaching. We can also see that his accomplishment is a group accomplishment, one that could not have occurred without every step of support from teacher and peers along the way. When we look at the work of Reggio children, we are often astonished at what they have accomplished (e.g., Vecchi, 2002). In the work of Mary Jane and other contributors in this book, we see this extraordinary capacity in children in our own school systems, when unhurried collaborative support is offered with delicacy, reciprocity, and perseverance.

CHAPTER 11

Toward a "Good-Enough" Theory of Emergent Curriculum

Carol Anne Wien

This chapter pulls together the classroom projects described by the contributors in order to create a generic map for emergent curriculum. The map is a kind of theory inasmuch as it makes sense as an organized landscape of emergent curriculum. It points to directions, choices teachers can make, and practices that support emergent curriculum. Anything creative, such as emergent curriculum, cannot be reduced to a formula or set pattern, for the pulse of life and alertness to the new must become part of it as it develops. So this map or theory of emergent curriculum is an attempt to understand the process of its creation without being formulaic.

Theory is a skeleton or framework, invisible but embedded within practice. All teaching practice has theory embedded within it, like the skeleton inside a mammal or the framing inside a house. Some aspects of theory are tacit, that is, hidden and not easily articulated, as I described in an earlier work (Wien, 1994), and some aspects teachers can consciously elaborate. In this chapter I will lay out the aspects of emergent curriculum that I see present in the contributors' chapters. I will relate what arises from this analysis to the "framework of five" outlined in Chapter 1, and I will show where that framework fits and whether more turns up than expected, or whether something disconfirms that framework. As I began writing this chapter, I could not see how it would turn out; thus I recognize this piece was my own emergent curriculum, as I carefully studied the work the teachers undertook. I am also conscious of the tension in my dual roles as teacher-mentor to the contributors, and researcher with an analysis agenda. Finally I will briefly consider the issue of the relation between standardized curriculum and emergent curriculum in schools.

STARTING POINTS IN EMERGENT CURRICULUM

There are aspects of emergent curriculum that are both stances toward children and their learning, and teaching practices, and it is impossible to separate the feeling tone of a stance from practice. Yet some things just seem necessary even to begin to consider emergent curriculum a possibility, and this section lays out those that occurred in the work of the contributors. These include an invitation to positive learning experiences, creating an opening for new possibilities, noticing topics of possible interest, a stance of doing things together, and allowing unhurried time.

Invitation to Positive Learning Experiences

There is in emergent curriculum a tone of emotion that is positive and expectant of creativity, ideas, and generation. Teachers expect this of themselves and of children, expect to take ownership of the content of study and offer their ideas, thoughts, imagined solutions, and possibilities to the situation at hand. This positive emotional stance sets a strong tone of invitation, of psychological safety that ideas are welcomed, that children belong to the group and have the right to participate in it. This stance creates in teachers a different feeling about teaching and learning than when they feel they must cover expectations. This positive tone of acceptance has a "flooring" or framework of many tacit values, such as children's right to participate, to offer their ideas in a respectful climate, to be safe both in body and spirit. Anyone can walk into such a classroom and recognize this atmosphere, a kind of "air" or ambience in which everyone is immersed. It is a kind of connective energy as is the air we breathe or the water fish swim in. There is in addition an expectant sense of the possibility of drawing from ourselves more than we knew was there. When Nancy Thomas (Chapter 2) drew music into her kindergarten classroom she found the rising excitement like "electricity," which she described as aliveness and alertness. Shaune Palmer (Chapter 3) and Brenda Jacobs (Chapter 7) speak about the engagement of the children in the chosen topic, and all the contributors notice the excitement and higher positive energy generated in the specific curriculum described. It is interesting that as this positive emotion grows so does children's persistence, until we see them laboring long and lovingly through extremely challenging obstacles, as in the case of Kang's horse (Chapter 10) or Sapphire's lightning (Chapter 9).

Creating an Opening for New Possibilities

An opening is a space/time into which we move, like an open door, or gateway, or bridge. If curriculum is prescripted, preplanned, and tightly controlled, the agenda for teaching and learning is closed. There is no opening for the new, the unexpected. To create an opening for new possibilities is to move away from confinement. Each teacher here found her own way to create an opening for herself and her children, consciously preparing a different "spatial landscape," different from normal school, in which something new might happen. They used a range of strategies to create these openings.

Selected group of children. Shaune Palmer and Brenda Jacobs used the strategy of selecting a small group of children (six to eight), for the context of a specific project. These children met together at set times and places for the work of their emergent curriculum.

Playtime. Nancy Thomas (Chapter 2) and Noula Berdoussis (Chapter 8) used a playtime of free-choice activities as the context from which to draw out the unexpected and creative. Their habit of noticing and watching across the whole group allowed them to select a focus of children's interest—music, sea creatures—that could gradually develop into more elaborate, detailed curriculum.

New material. Vanessa Barnett and Deborah Halls (Chapter 5) used the context of a new material—wire—explored across many classroom activities, as the vehicle for creating their opening into new possibilities for Deborah's children. Nancy Thomas's expansion of music activities and Mary Jane Miller's (Chapter 10) welcome of weaving are other examples.

A problem to explore. Susan Hislop and Jennifer Armstrong (Chapter 7), and Mary Jane Miller (Chapter 10) used the context of a problem as the opening. For Susan and Jennifer it was the proposal for flower boxes that provided the opening into elaborate problem solving. Mary Jane brought a boy's interest in imagining a woven horse into the curriculum where his problem could be explored and theorized.

Dedicated time. Diana Will (Chapter 9) created a time frame inserted into her weekly schedule when she and her children attempted a different kind of teaching and learning. She found they all had to learn habits of mind and action in this inquiry time that were different from normal schooling; with her particular group that alone required 4 months.

Creating a time, creating a place, creating a small group, an exploration with new material, following a problem or question—these were the ways this group of teachers and principals created openings into new possibilities. Because time and space in schools are fully scheduled and fully occupied, curriculum can only emerge in schools when there is a consciously prepared opening that invites it.

Noticing: Creating a Figure-Ground Distinction

Something has to be lifted out of the rapid-fire stream of teaching experience to be noticed and reflected upon. I liken the capacity to notice to the capacity to distinguish a figure against a background: If we can see the figure we can consider it; if it remains part of the backdrop, it passes us by. Nancy Thomas lifted out from the backdrop of play in her classroom the children's making of little instruments, then chided herself because it took her so long to consider doing something about it. She recognized that the possibility existed without her noticing it for several months. Then she saw it. Vanessa Barnett and Deborah Halls noticed the children's interest in bicycles and linked that spring activity with the new material they wished to explore. Susan Hislop noticed the children's immediate desire to count plants when faced with a measurement problem, and this incongruity sent her into a tizzy of self-reflection on her teaching and an investigation of children's understanding. Noula Berdoussis noticed the children role-playing starfish and the excited response to comments about them in conversation. Diana Will noticed a child who could not engage with inquiry and was propelled into teacher action. Mary Jane Miller noticed an incredible question—"Can weaving make a horse?"— that she lifted out of the teaching landscape to take seriously.

Noticing in the mind can be compared to perception by the senses. Just as we can walk by a treed slope and not see the oaks among the maples, thoughts about children's learning have to push their way into our consciousness before we can take them up. Actions, words, and work by the children all stream over us in the midst of daily teaching experience like a waterfall. It is difficult to describe noticing, but without that shimmer of possibility around something that the teacher senses has potential so that she consciously leans toward it, what could possibly emerge?

Doing Things Together

In traditional teaching, teachers give instructions to children about what to do, and the children (preferably) do it. In emergent curriculum, teachers and children together decide what to do and teachers participate in learning alongside children, asking their own questions and conducting their own quest. Because it is such a different stance toward learning than in traditional styles of teaching, teachers and children find there is an adjustment period while the group finds its feet in this way of learning. Leadership moves around, variety of roles increases, and participation and responsibility for work increase because they are initiated by the learner in response to real questions. It is a small cooperative movement within a classroom community. The unit on the city (Chapter 4) shows how ill at ease the children were initially with the new structure, how the teachers added more structure to refine group functioning, and how even by the end of one week, the children showed enthusiasm to initiate and carry their own learning forward. Nancy Thomas's music story and Noula Berdoussis's starfish story show how a topic for serious consideration as curriculum can be teased out from the complex activities generated by children in play. In Diana Will's case, it took longer—4 months— to settle most of her children into an inquiry mode, and these were the least resourced children, in terms of literacy and numeracy scores, in a high-needs school. Her story gives compelling evidence that even the children considered least likely to succeed can experience powerful learning using emergent curriculum.

Unhurried Time

All the contributors noted the necessity of slowing down in schools to engage with emergent curriculum in a steadier way. Perhaps we should call emergent curriculum part of a "slow learning" movement, parallel with slow cooking or slow dressing. Unhurried time is ecologically sound in that it respects children's own pace in activity, giving them sufficient time and space to experience satisfaction and permit an organic close to activities. Of course teachers attempting to get off the production schedule organization of time in schools face enormous difficulties from highly scheduled bureaucratic processes of controlling time. Yet each contributor here found a way to create such a space and time, if only for a week;

though for some, like Brenda Jacobs, it also meant making difficult choices like using gym or music time for group research sessions. Others carved out large blocks of uninterrupted time several times per week and created new practice within that time frame.

Unhurried time also means permitting children to repeat activities and providing them opportunity to choose to do so. Many sketches of bicycles or cars or the sun and moon are needed to persist in thinking and theorizing. Though much of adult life is short and fast, big problems and big design projects require sustained attention, persistence, and endurance. Everything from designing opera houses to Internet programs, from writing books to government reports, from designing new structures in universities to on-reserve housing, requires years of stubborn persistence, hope, and positive energy. Children who have participated in projects in unhurried time have had some experience and practice both with the emotional and intellectual demands and also with what it feels like to put the project, rather than the routine schedule, first. Thus an aspect of unhurried time requires adults to refrain from changing topics, from abrupt transitions to other activities, and from imposing competing demands for children's involvement. Within unhurried time, there is room for a child to take a break when tired, to breathe out in relaxation before taking up the task again. These rhythms are necessary to all intense work—how often do I get up and walk around as I write this chapter, or go make another cup of tea—and the one doing the work must set the pace to get it done. Vanessa Barnett and Deborah Halls refer to unhurried time as children permitted to be "masters of their own timing."

PARTICIPATORY STRUCTURES AND STANCES

Emergent curriculum is all about teachers sharing power with learners. I am uncomfortable using the term *letting go* to describe the sense of loosening the reins of control of the teaching agenda because it hides the fact that there are powerful structures that undergird and sustain emergent curriculum; just standing back does not make it happen. This section describes some of the scaffolding strategies I see the contributors using that provide structures of participation, rather than authoritarian control, in classrooms.

Listening with Care

Whether we call it "participatory consciousness" (Heshusius, 1994) or a "pedagogy of listening" (Rinaldi, 1998), all the teachers here place a strong value on listening with care to others, attending to the development of thought, and trying to understand it. Such listening invites others to speak. But the listening also includes openness to the response, an acceptance of what is said. Such acceptance means the speaker feels valued and acknowledged. If what is offered is neither declined nor corrected, the learner feels welcome to speak. (As in any other setting, negative or unethical behavior toward others would be addressed.). Bruner (1996) describes intersubjectivity as "Mutually figuring out what others have in mind" (p. 117). *Subjectivity* is our experience, and our awareness of it. *Intersubjectivity* is sharing and studying this experience. It is like the experience of role play, where we take the perspective of another or "walk in their shoes," as the cliché says, except that here we walk beside the other. The Reggio educators have shown us that when a collaborative group takes on this quality of close listening to the other, the ethical, intellectual, and affective qualities of the work grow so extraordinary it merits world attention. In this book, we catch glimpses of what such group attentiveness can create. All the contributors show listening with care; and the contributors to Part II, Susan Hislop, Brenda Jacobs, Noula Berdoussis, Diana Will, and Mary Jane Miller show strong qualities of participatory consciousness in their work to grasp what children mean—sometimes they convince children to work hard at this too. The depth of thinking they captured in their own research allows us to see the children's thinking develop.

Providing Entry Points

An entry point is something singular that provides direction and focus to the learner, who is entering the unknown territory of new learning. In instances where learners do not know how to begin, teachers lead by offering words, or materials, or physical presence, to help the learner take action. Diana placed a "fancy pencil" and paper in Sapphire's inquiry bin, suggesting writing. Mary Jane asked Kang, "Two cardboard pieces or one for the body?"—just enough to get him going.

Offering a Bridge of Attachment

The bridge of attachment is an emotional connection the teacher makes with a child that acts as a link between the child and her learning. Diana shows us how important it was for Sapphire that her teacher loved her question. The teacher's affective response became a proxy fuel that motivated Sapphire to get started in inquiry. I say a proxy fuel, because it was necessary for the child to have the "loan" of this positive energy before she would work well enough to gain positive satisfaction from the work on her own. With belief and emotional energy loaned from her teacher, Sapphire could begin and slowly build intense interest and self-sustained motivation that carried her inquiry through multiple pencil sketches and paintings. We can see how this bridge of attachment helps to carry the child outward into new possibilities of accomplishment and identity. I think this bridge of attachment has two aspects: the long, slow buildup of positive regard and belief in capacity; and a moment of release that sets things in motion. Diana's love of Sapphire's question was the quick spark that ignited her inquiry. We see the slow, steady phase also in Brenda's story, where the children's collaborative engagement with a difficult question continued for 35 sessions, at their insistence. It is an energy that the learner can ride on as they begin, and it is, I think, the beginning of the windhorse effect.

Choosing Learning Opportunities

Providing learners with the opportunity to choose what to do gives them ownership and responsibility for their learning. With ownership comes engagement.

Having some room to decide what to do in school creates positive fuel for the times when there is no choice. Having a landscape with freedom to choose gives children practice in thinking through alternatives and making a choice. It is an act of the imagination to preview alternatives and make a good selection. What better training for future voting? Choice of activity was a predominant aspect of all the emergent curriculum described here. In fact, in Diana's story, a child's difficulty in making meaningful choices became the "cognitive knot" for the teacher. Clearly teachers must provide sufficient scaffolding—in the design of the environment, in the variety of materials available as choice, in the handling of time to allow real activity, in finding entry points for specific children—so that choice is meaningful. But once children learn how to choose from a range of possibilities, teachers learn from children's choices what their interests and intentions are. Then real engagement in education begins.

Joining Children in Activity

Participation by children was sometimes supported when teachers joined children's activity in a way that is unusual in schools. Noula "purchased" a shell from the children who were playing store in her class, and gave the shell a place in the classroom, opening up children's notions of how materials could be moved around and related to other objects used in the classroom. Her action sparked new and playful interest in shells and the ocean. Diana, in joining Sapphire to role-play lightning, gave the child the confidence that this was a legitimate way to imagine and think, and out of their perspective taking rose a new connection and question for this child. To have a principal join children's activity, as Shaune did, is most unusual, and a powerful incentive to participate. The participation of a principal sets a tone for the entire school community.

DESIGN WORK

Emergent curriculum involves children and teachers in designing something new. Whether it be their own musical instruments, a car-racing derby, a wire bicycle, a flower-box garden, black space picture, clay structures that show the birth of starfish, lightning paintings, or Kang's horse, after emergent curriculum there is something new in the world that was not present before it. Emergent curriculum involves creative design work. Nor was the newly made planned at the outset. What was created grew out of the organic process of interaction and collaboration among people and materials. The range in quality of design is wide, from the primitive musical instruments made of taped boxes to the highly elaborated wire bicycle sculpture or woven horse. Sometimes the design aspect involved insightful problem solving, as in a child's suggestion of a metronome to measure speed or in a girl's suggestion of tiles to measure areas of plants. Sometimes it created probable lasting contributions to children's identity and sense of belonging, as in the construction of the wire bicycle, the woven horse, or the flower boxes that remain as a feature of the playground.

Real Experience

In school much learning is mediated through text and representation, but in emergent curriculum children and teachers step out into real experience, real stuff, real problems—learning lived in three dimensions. An aspect of design work is that it is based in the real. Susan's children were making real jewelry for a family member. Noula and Alice (Chapter 4) took children out into the city for a real encounter. Children and teachers can experience the real without design work, but design work always engages the real. Nancy brought in real musical instruments to explore. Susan's girls were measuring family members for jewelry and later in the year measuring plants, both complex three-dimensional organic objects. And their attempts to measure flower boxes were real measurements that would matter to others in their school. A sense of responsibility to others may accompany design work.

I believe design work is central to emergent curriculum. Enormous satisfaction and identity development occurs for children and teachers through arriving at a satisfactory design, whether of a lightning painting or flower boxes on a playground. Design requires imagining possibilities, but also engaging with the very real affordances (Forman, 1996) or properties of materials.

Real Problems

As soon as complex design projects emerge, both teachers and learners engage very real problems, from a toy guitar made from a cardboard box to measuring flower boxes for the school. The specific problems arise out of the properties of the materials used in interaction with the intentions of the designer. Valeska wanted to build vertically with clay, which is heavy and unstable and Noula (Chapter 8) feared the problems would be insurmountable. Cars with axles in the wrong place go round in circles instead of fast. Plants are a challenge to measure, for measurement is geometric and plants organic. And lightning is an elemental phenomenon impossible to hold still for study.

Invitations to Draw and Redraw

Teachers here treated drawing as an important vehicle for learning. They frequently invited children to draw in order to expand their thinking and learning. I found invitations to draw and redraw were used repeatedly and served several purposes. Drawing from observation was used to expand children's awareness of detail and structure, and to sharpen perception: Teachers in Nancy's school, for instance, were astonished at the detail in the children's observational drawings of the guitar. Second, drawing was used as a way to make plans. Mary Jane used drawing repeatedly to help Kang think through his design for his horse, and her children themselves suggested drawing their plans for how to make his horse move. Third, drawing was used as a vehicle for developing ideas and theories. Sapphire used it as her entry point to understanding the motion of lightning, a complex and ephemeral phenomenon difficult to study. Noula's children used drawing to depict their theories of how the starfish ray grows back when cut off. Brenda used drawing as a vehicle for expressing understanding of planetary relationships. Drawing was also used as a map by Shaune's group to diagram their ramps and measurements. Drawing as a route to learning more is highly evident as a strategy used by teachers developing emergent curriculum.

Openness to Many Graphic Materials

In addition to drawing, the teachers offered a wide variety of graphic materials for children to explore. Nancy might never have known the appeal of instruments to her children if she had not provided a space with construction possibilities with tape, glue, and scissors. Mary Jane's invitation of weaving into the classroom included a technology seldom acknowledged in schools. Vanessa and Deborah's introduction of wire and large-scale sculpture with metal were also new technologies for learning. The teachers included clay, wire, light, weaving, painting, and pastels in addition to drawing, and these varied materials expanded interest, bodily awareness, and sensory investigation, all of which are highly desirable for the healthy development of young children (Bredekamp & Copple, 1997).

Artists Expand Pedagogy

Artists, when carefully selected for work with children and teachers, change pedagogies in schools by bringing their knowledge of design, their expertise with materials, and their specific aesthetic sensibilities to education (Wien & Callaghan, 2007). It is rare for children to have extensive experience with three dimensional materials in schools where so much knowledge is text based and semantically organized. Note that all the teachers here were offering three dimensional experiences to their children, from Brenda's role play of planetary movement to Noula and Alice's field trip into the city center, and many encouraged children to make things in three dimensions. Our sole example here of an artist working within a classroom shows how the knowledge that Vanessa brings as an artist allows several things to happen. She uses space in three-dimensional ways, so that after the initial wire exploration there is a branch suspended from the ceiling, hung with tiny beaded wire shapes. It changes the air, the upper space of the classroom, bringing it texture and sparkle. She changes the scale of activity, inviting children to draw a bicycle that is life-size. This allows the child to enter the drawing, for it extends beyond peripheral vision. Then combining three-dimensional work with large-scale work requires the children to "think big." The process is expansive, opening out into the world. To see the wire bicycle sculpture hung in the air and their full-scale drawings behind it is to see bicycles in new ways. It also shows layers of children's activity present in the classroom. The environment indeed begins to have its capacity as a third teacher. The combination of complex processes and their interconnections—real bicycle, real new materials to explore (wire), enlarging scale with projected images, combining full-scale work with 3-D materials— expands learning experience and results in extended pedagogy beyond normal teaching. While emergent curriculum can be created without the participation of artists, the highest level accomplishments of Reggio children are clearly affected by the design and creativity support made possible by the *atelieristi* working in their schools, such as Giovanni Piazza's support for *An Amusement Park for Birds* (Forman & Gandini, 1994) or Vea Vecchi's for the curtain in the Ariosto Theater (Vecchi, 2002).

PROPELLING LEARNING: TEACHER RESEARCH AND PEDAGOGICAL DOCUMENTATION

How is curriculum developed when it is emergent and not planned from the outset? If a teacher has established participatory structures and stances for collaboration in her room, has put in place recognized starting points for emergent curriculum, has included wide use of graphic materials and possibilities for design work, all of these processes contribute to a lively healthy classroom community. But what then?

I argue that teacher research is the driving force that propels emergent curriculum. By that I refer to the teachers' quest to understand or explore or investigate that gives the topic its broad direction. Susan's quest to understand the girls' notion of measurement, Noula and Alice's quest to try a different sort of pedagogy during the unit on the city, Diana's to draw a child into relationship with inquiry— all begin with teachers' need to understand and create. And if the teacher understands what it is like to have an inquiry and follow it through to provisional answers, then it is possible to cultivate the same stance in children. With a direction set by an intentional desire to understand or create, what then do teachers do?

Conversations to Understand What Others Think

Talking to grasp thinking. Listening with care—being attuned to the other— when modeled by teachers, helps set up collaborative contexts in which children work together on a problem. A conversation here does not mean a social chit-chat with freedom to say anything, but a focused context of searching together for what the group thinks or theorizes in reference to a specific topic. Frequently, we do not know what we think until we create a gap or space in which to examine our thoughts. When we create this gap with others and try out our thoughts, we can see thought develop. Several teachers noted it was the first time they had a conversation of this depth and watched themselves relinquishing control of the movement of thought, opening up to the fact they did not know what the children would say.

Questions as seeds to thinking. Noula and Alice, in their city unit, saw that the children required a more structured focus for their attention and chose to use questions. But the questions were of a different type—Reggio-influenced—than those frequently used in schools, for they were neither open (allowing any response, as in social chat) nor closed (requiring an answer the teacher already knows), but rather they invited the children to think their own thoughts, generate theories, and hypothesize possibilities around a chosen topic. The quality of reflecting on what we think led me to use the phrase "questions as seeds to thinking," a way for teachers to provoke or probe more focused thinking in children. When teachers speak of "letting go" (e.g., Jones & Nimmo, 1994), one of the things to let go of is an expectation of a desired response; yet teachers are still responsible for supporting children in focusing their thinking. Diana used her own capacity to question as an exemplar for her puzzled children, encouraging them to experience questions through her example and to develop a new habit of mind. Susan, Noula, Diana, and Mary Jane all show the habit of asking probing questions that can seed thinking.

Highlighting conflicts in thinking. Noula consciously brought together for discussion two boys who had contrasting theories about starfish, one boy thinking they had bones and another who thought they were "jelly." Within a context of established collaborative relationship, she put forth this conflict and invited them to consider it. Her documentation makes visible a child in the process of changing his thinking, a most valuable moment of transformation in education.

Inviting theorizing. The chapters in Part II show children invited to consider various possibilities within their topic and to invent theories that they might then consider. Inventing a theory makes children want to find out whether such a possibility could be true and drives them to seek out answers. Such efforts assist children and teachers in grasping the difference between an idea in mind and a recognized reality in the world, so that distinctions between our interpretations of reality and that reality itself become possible. This is sophisticated understanding. Often adults themselves believe that what they think of the world must be true because they think it, when much of our acceptance of reality is interpretive. To begin to cultivate this distinction in young children is a profound service to the development of thought in a society.

Pedagogical Documentation

Documentation is the process that allows a "pedagogy of listening" to be place-held for consideration by others: it lifts thinking out of the stream of lived experience in education and makes it visible. When a train goes by at high speed, all we can do is count cars; when education is fast paced and rushed, all we can do is measure. When the train stops, we can consider many other aspects: who gets on and off, what freight is carried, the arrangements for food. Suddenly it is a dynamic system with interconnections to many parts of society. Pedagogical documentation stops the train of standardized expectations and slows down our thinking processes to consider some topic with exquisite care. It is a different technology for studying education.

The habits of documenting. In order to document, teachers must first develop the habits of documenting so that they become automatic. Because of early childhood education's focus on close observation and anecdotal records, this habit is comfortable for many teachers, if new to others. Documenting habits require that teachers grow accustomed to having recording devices on hand—whether digital or video camera, audiotaping device, or notepads and pen—but some form of place-holding information has to be in place to capture something for future study. A worthy goal for teachers who want to begin pedagogical documentation is to concentrate on developing the habit of documenting. But what should be documented? That depends on what is noticed, making the figure-ground distinction that pulls out something to follow.

Composing documentation. When she has piles of audiotaped and transcribed bits of conversations, oodles of digital images or video, and children's work before her, what does a teacher do then? (I find many teachers can get this far, but find it difficult to do more because of time constraints.) What does she do with this material? First, she thinks: What is she looking for? What does she want to make visible? Who is the documentation for? Decisions about these issues help her sift and sort her mountains of material to choose just the few images, pieces of sample work, spoken text, and so forth that highlight her intentions. If she has colleagues with whom to make these decisions, the analysis will be more time-consuming but also more closely vetted and reassuring because it is shared. Once the materials are chosen to fit her intentions, the next step is to decide how they should be displayed to communicate these intentions to others. What layout, what use of blank space, what sizes and format, contribute to support those intentions? This process is excessively time-consuming; teachers have to believe it is worth the effort. But when shared with parents, the excitement in parents shifts attention from scores. A visit to the Reggio exhibit with its profound sharing of the lives, thinking, and feeling of Reggio children and the beautiful sensibility with which their voices are shared, renews our faith in the power of pedagogical documentation to create change in ourselves and in education.

Revisiting documentation. Where documentation is part of the stream of classroom life, teachers find children fascinated by seeing their words ("I said that?") and work processes made visible to others. The children grasp that teachers value their ideas and value the intentional quest they have set. Contributors here found children looking over documentation on their own, explaining it to others, and excited when new documentation appeared. It is like having movie stills of our own lives around us. This visibility of thought and feeling provokes reflection and sharpens the mind.

Among the contributors here, Susan and Jennifer, Noula, and Mary Jane in particular were sufficiently developed in their skills of pedagogical documentation to use it as a process to propel curriculum. In concert with strategies mentioned under the section on conversations above, the process of revisiting and rethinking what is happening in the work, through studying documentation, leads to new thoughts, connections, and possibilities for planning curriculum. Documentation slows down and place-holds thinking for consideration.

Studying and interpreting documentation. When adults (parents, teachers, visitors) engage closely with documentation, they find it stimulates thought, impresses them with the unexpected reach of children's minds, and offers new ways of engaging with children's learning. Quite simply, outsiders get involved. Reggio has shown a genius for disseminating its approach (while insisting it is not a model to copy, but an exchange of cultures), and this genius has been pedagogical documentation. No other program that we know has developed such metacognitive awareness about what they are doing, and no other worldwide program has been under such intense scrutiny for the last 35 years.

When adults study pedagogical documentation closely and share their interpretations, these turn out to be multiple, sometimes startlingly different. Documentation then becomes a vehicle for considering multiple perspectives. Engagement, excited thinking, conversing, and possible planning all occur. Susan and Jennifer's chapter concentrates on mathematical thinking, so that the process of studying documentation is not so visible, but it undergirds their chapter. Noula and Mary Jane show us how the documentation was used as a focal point for communication and conversation in small groups and how that focus of attention contributed ideas for plans of action.

Documentation as a spur to planning. While we readily recognize that teachers generate plans from reviewing documentation, as Shaune describes, it is amazing to see the concept of documenting in order to plan taken up spontaneously by children. When Mary Jane drew a small group of children together to consider what Kang should do to make his woven horse move, the children had many spontaneous ideas and, accustomed to the process of collaborative problem solving, themselves suggested documenting their ideas and plans for Kang so he could remember them. The five plans they made were so detailed, beautiful, and lovingly done, that Kang studied them for 4 weeks, going over them repeatedly, before arriving at his own plan that drew from all of theirs. We can see that his finished horse could not have been made as it was without the collaborative efforts of the small group. Mary Jane and I loved the fact the children took on the effort of documenting their plans themselves.

Embracing Uncertainty, Persisting Through Obstacles

A problem, a conflict, a tension between two things is troubling to us; we want to avoid it. But these chapters show that persisting through obstacles and problems supports emergent curriculum and that this quality of persistence in the face of difficulty and uncertainty results in high-quality work. In emergent curriculum, as in life, events show up which stop us in our tracks: We do not know how to respond because this specific event has never arisen before like this. It is unclear what move will bring a positive result, and the term *knot* seems a good image for the tangle of confusion teachers experience. The Reggio phrase "cognitive knot" (Rinaldi, 1998) is helpful in imaging an intellectual problem. Keating, a master teacher of emergent curriculum in a child care setting, says the problem "gives a direction" (Wien, Keating & Coates, in press). It tells her where to focus attention and direct her energy. Perceived as a direction, the knot is like a labyrinth that has a way in and possibly several ways out. Posing a problem establishes a landscape of possible creativity. It is, in part, the setting or finding of the problem that allows the creativity necessary for its solution to occur. Susan's "cognitive knot" was the fact that the girls were counting rather than measuring, sparking intense small-group work in which she was careful not to force the issue. Shaune's "cognitive knot" was the fact that the children were measuring distance but referred consistently to speed. Something in their understanding was confused. As she explored the difficulty, she opened up the discussion about speed and distance and the children found a brilliant solution to address their interest—the metronome. Diana showed extraordinary persistence and fortitude in persisting through 4 months of settling her class into inquiry and then the additional time to engage Sapphire. Mary Jane had many moments of challenge in trying to grasp what Kang was thinking, and in the technical challenges of weaving a three-dimensional object. Throughout Part II of this book we see example after example of this persisting through obstacles, from a horse that looks like a dinosaur to children that insist starfish have bones.

There is another way uncertainty is embraced. That is in a teacher's refusal to limit her notions of what children can accomplish. In compelling examples of emergent curriculum, we see an expansive view of imagination in teachers. Present here in many forms, this view is exemplified by Diana and Mary Jane's conscious articulation. Diana said, "I did not want to limit her imagination by what she thought she could and could not do well." Mary Jane said, "I don't want Kang to limit his imagination by what he thinks he can and cannot do." In both cases, we see the teacher believing in the capability of the child and permitting a reach far ahead of current functioning. That's the bridge of attachment, that embrace of uncertain possibilities, that flying energy that gives us all hope when someone believes in us and what we might do.

Embedding Standardized Curriculum Within Emergent Curriculum

Several chapters in this book highlighted the interrelation of emergent curriculum and specific outcomes detailed in standardized curriculum. Both Shaune (Chapter 3), and Noula and Alice (Chapter 4) begin with a unit described in standardized curriculum and use that foundation to open the work into richer possibilities by bringing Reggio-inspired processes into the context. Both are interested in the notion of children as protagonists taking ownership of action and learning, and both set up the learning environment in such a way that they can permit the children and their voices to step forward. Both are intrigued by collaboration and invite collegial learning into the mix. Both were watching carefully to ensure that specific expectations required by the unit were accomplished. Both describe how readily they were accomplished, yet in a way that resulted, they felt, in deeper and more connected learning that would remain memorable.

A difficulty with standardized curriculum can be the coercive force it has on teachers, and their beliefs about how they must approach it. The force of documents written in linear lists of expectations or outcomes frequently leads teachers to the interpretation that outcomes must be taught item by item. I have written elsewhere (Wien, 2004b) about this interesting and unintentional aspect of standardized curriculum. In addition, many teachers fear that if they do not address expectations explicitly, then those expectations are not present in their program: They miss the fact that much learning is layered and tacit. The explicit and direct instruction of a linear, fragmented approach is one way to teach a standardized curriculum. For young children it is not the best approach, for it contravenes the research knowledge bases of child development and neuroscience.

Another way to teach standardized curriculum is to embed it in richer, more integrated processes such as emergent curriculum, where its presence can be documented to make it visible, rather than being measured on tests. If these processes are carefully documented then measurement is not necessary, as the data clearly show learning without transforming it into a metaphorical number. But the question of how emergent curriculum and standardized curriculum might interrelate is merely suggested in this book, and requires a different research project and another book, if it were to be studied seriously: It would be a useful continuation of the discussion. It is a limitation of our book that we did not do more with this issue, but it was not the central or intended focus.

When I consider the "framework of five" in Chapter 1, I see that my description of "the discipline of self-regulating groups" has become folded into what I describe in this chapter as participatory stances and structures. We can see that emergent curriculum is a different way of teaching and learning that requires all participants to learn its democratic structures, for it demands that participants become citizens of a group or community with well-developed concern for one another. This is very different from the individual competitiveness of a standardized system. Because emergent curriculum demands group support and group thinking, it requires teachers and children to think of others, to try to understand them. I am reminded of the nursery rhyme "Humpty Dumpty": I fear that taking up a standardized curriculum in linear, fragmented ways is like living with a broken Humpty that cannot be put together again for all our efforts. But approaching standardized curriculum in other ways, of which emergent curriculum is one, *does* permit us to educate by building connections and studying the connectivity of living systems in a respectful, ethical way. Bateson (1979) argued that it is the understanding of the connectedness among all things in the world that matters in learning. He was speaking of evolutionary biology when he said:

> Break the pattern that connects the items of learning and you necessarily destroy all quality. (p. 8)

At the risk of overgeneralizing, it is my interpretation that breaking the pattern that connects, in anyone's learning, reduces the possibility of quality education, and the pattern that connects is the pattern that learners find in their quest to understand. I argue that emergent curriculum is a route by which to restore connectivity in education. I speculate that, in fact, it may be the restoration of full connectivity to all processes of living that results in the fifth aspect of emergent curriculum that we see arise, the dynamic emotional and psychic energy that I call *windhorse.*

THE WINDHORSE EFFECT

Let me tell you a new story, rather than repeat what you have heard before. This story concerns adults creating our own emergent curriculum to further understanding. During the months that the Reggio exhibit, "The Hundred Languages of Children," visited Toronto, the organizing committee developed many events as professional development opportunities for educators and the public. When it came time to organize the closing conference, and we considered who we might invite to speak, one member said, "What's been missing in all this is the chance to go deeper" into the exhibit. I responded that if we wanted to go deeper, we had to do less, not more. Out of that exchange, we organized two one-day events that invited participants to engage seriously with the exhibit and then to create, with the support of artists and facilitators, something from materials that spoke to their connection to the exhibit and the relation they felt with it. The artists chose the materials they would use—wire, corrugated cardboard, leftover industrial plastics, collage, light and shadow—and we tried to craft the day as an occasion of unhurried time in which to engage with and reflect on the exhibit, by making something. At the end of the day we came together in the middle of the rotunda beneath the Reggio exhibit with an echo exhibit of our own, and participants spoke about their creations.

It was a moving and incredible process both days, with a team of 15 of us engaging in and supporting the collaborative effort, and participants astonished both by what they created and by listening to others and seeing their creations. The conference team's belief was that it is impossible for teachers to help children create unless they themselves have had multiple opportunities to design and create; we saw our task in part was to offer such opportunity. Many teachers, when describing their creation, spoke of their heartbreak in schools over what they are required to do with children in relation to testing, and their sense of its destructiveness. They spoke of how the conference process gave them hope, a sense of freedom but also of responsibility, how "we didn't want to finish, we wanted to keep going."

Two examples give a sense of the work produced and shared among the group. Wendy Gilchrist, who worked with corrugated cardboard, placed a huge boxlike contraption with a front roller on display and spoke about how it was the Zamboni machine, the machine that resurfaces the ice between periods in a hockey game. She described how Reggio ideas were so unusual and challenging that she felt they were changing the very functioning of her brain. "I have to resurface my brain, resurface my old way of thinking" just as the Zamboni machine resurfaces the ice. Wendy said:

> The biggest resurfacing of my brain deals with my image of the child and my role as a teacher. I see children so differently now. It is so true that I would have left the field if I had not had the Reggio inspiration. I have been in the field for more than 20 years and my greatest growth has been in the last five years, and being part of a Reggio-inspired program.

FIGURE 11.1. Ruggero Racca's sculpture *The Roots That Unite Us,* showing the connection between Reggio Emilia and our North American contexts.

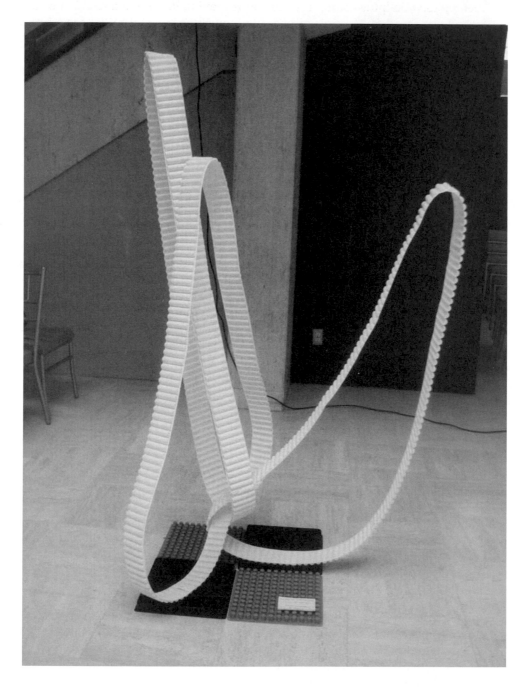

A second example is the work of Ruggero Racca, who said he was applying to a Master of Teaching program. He created from white and black plastic industrial rectangles, a sculpture of three arced forms moving in a wave through the air, and suspended this from a spiral staircase so it hung before us. Visually it was stunning, easily recognized as a work of art (see Figure 11.1), and he stunned us further when he spoke. His voice choked as he thanked us for a space of beauty and quiet in which to think and share. He said it had been a most unusual conference, full of layers of intimacy, and then spoke of his sculpture title as *The Roots That Unite Us*. As an Italian himself, he appreciated the power of the Reggio ideas to illuminate educators in Toronto, as in many other places, and was grateful for this connection.

I share this story of the conference because to me it illustrates the windhorse effect of rising positive energy, joy, thoughtfulness, the sense of giving to the world through positive forces, and because it is my own attempt to join the contributors in the book by sharing an example of emergent curriculum for which I, with others, was responsible. When people visit Reggio on study tours, they often fall in love with a way of being, and want to create and sustain it for themselves, their programs, and children and families back home. The approach calls up a connecting identity in others, a desire to make teaching and learning more beautiful, shared, responsive to children's voices and concerns, more creative and loving. This book is a first step in showing the values of relationality, reciprocity, and collaboration in schools, of inviting children and teachers to be protagonists of their own teaching and learning and of creating emergent curriculum that propels learning and sustains community. We thank the community of Reggio Emilia for its profound inspiration and generous sharing of their culture with others, and we celebrate the appearance of our own interpretations, on a windhorse of new energy, in public elementary schools.

References

Ashton-Warner, S. A. (1963). *Teacher*. New York: Simon and Shuster.

Audet, R. H., & Jordan, L. K. (Eds.). (2005). *Integrating inquiry across the curriculum.* Thousand Oaks, CA: Corwin Press.

Bateson, G. (1979). *Mind and nature: A necessary unity.* New York: Dutton.

Booth, D., & Hachiya, M. (2004). *The arts go to school: Classroom-based activities that focus on music, painting, drama, movement, media, and more.* Markham, Ontario: Pembroke.

Bredekamp, S., & Copple, C. (Eds.). (1997). *Developmentally appropriate practice in early childhood programs.* (Rev. ed.). Washington, DC: National Association for the Education of Young Children.

Bruner, J. (1960). *The process of education.* Cambridge, MA: Harvard University Press.

Bruner, J. (1996). A little city miracle. In L. Malaguzzi (Ed.), *The hundred languages of children: Narrative of the possible* [Catalog of the exhibit]. Reggio Emilia, Italy: Reggio Children.

Cadwell, L. B. (1997). *Bringing Reggio Emilia home: An innovative approach to early childhood education.* New York: Teachers College Press.

Cadwell, L. B. (2003). *Bringing learning to life: The Reggio approach to early childhood education.* New York: Teachers College Press.

Caine, R. N., & Caine, G. (1997). *Education on the edge of possibility.* Alexandria, VA: Association for Supervision and Curriculum Development.

Cannon, J. (1993). *Stellaluna.* New York: Harcourt Brace.

Capra, F. (2002). *The hidden connections: A science for sustainable living.* New York: Anchor/Random.

Chapin, S., & Johnson, A. (2000). *Math makes sense: Understanding the math you teach, grades K–6.* Sausalito, CA: Math Solutions.

Csikszentmihalyi, M. (1990). *Flow: The psychology of optimal experience.* New York: Harper & Row.

Dahlberg, G., Moss, P., & Pence, A. (1999). *Beyond quality in early childhood education and care: Postmodern perspectives.* London: Falmer Press.

Dahlberg, G. & Moss, P. (2006). Introduction to our Reggio Emilia. In C. Rinaldi, *In dialogue with Reggio Emilia: Listening, researching and learning.* New York: Routledge.

Davis, B., & Sumara, D. (1997). Cognition, complexity, and teacher education. *Harvard Educational Review, 67*(1), 105-125.

Dewey, J. (1933). *How we think: A restatement of the relation of reflective thinking to the educative process.* Boston: D. C. Heath.

Duckworth, E. (1996). *"The having of wonderful ideas" and other essays on teaching and learning.* New York: Teachers College Press.

Edwards, C. (1998). Partner, nurturer, and guide: The role of the teacher. In C. Edwards, L. Gandini, & G. Forman (Eds.), *The hundred languages of children: The Reggio Emilia approach—advanced reflections* (pp. 179–198). Greenwich, CT: Ablex.

Edwards, C., Gandini, L., & Forman, G. (Eds.). (1998). *The hundred languages of children: The Reggio Emilia Approach—advanced reflections.* Greenwich, CT: Ablex.

Ehrlert, L. (1990). *Fish eyes: A counting book*. San Diego: Harcourt Brace Jovanovich.

Eisner, E. (1997). *The enlightened eye: Qualitative inquiry and the enhancement of educational practice* (2nd Ed.). New York: Merrill.

Filippini, T. (1998). The role of the pedagogista. In C. Edwards, L. Gandini, & G. Forman (Eds.), *The hundred languages of children: The Reggio Emilia approach—advanced reflections* (pp. 127–137). Greenwich, CT: Ablex.

Florian, D. (2000). *A pig is big*. New York: Greenville Books.

Forman, G. (1996). Negotiating with art media to deepen learning. *Child Care Information Exchange, 10*(8), 56–58.

Forman, G., & Fyfe, B. (1998). Negotiated learning through design, documentation, and discourse. In C. Edwards, L. Gandini, & G. Forman (Eds.), *The hundred languages of children: The Reggio Emilia approach, advanced reflections* (pp. 239–260). Greenwich, CT: Ablex.

Forman, G., & Gandini, L. (Eds.). (1994). *An amusement park for birds*. [Video recording.] Amherst, MA: Performanetics.

Forman, G., Lee, M., Wrisley, L., & Langley, J. (1993). The city in the snow: Applying the multisymbolic approach in Massachusetts. In C. Edwards, L. Gandini, & G. Forman (Eds.), *The hundred languages of children: The Reggio Emilia approach to early childhood education* (pp. 233–250). Norwood, NJ: Ablex.

Franklin, U. (1999). *The real world of technology* (Rev. ed). Toronto: Anansi.

Gallas, K. (1994). *The languages of learning: How children talk, write, dance, draw, and sing their understanding of the world*. New York: Teachers College Press.

Gallas, K. (1995). *Talking their way into science: Hearing children's questions and theories, responding with curricula*. New York: Teachers College Press.

Gallas, K. (2003). *Imagination and literacy: A teacher's search for the heart of teaching*. New York: Teachers College Press.

Gambetti, A. (2004, June). The Reggio Emilia approach to early childhood education. Conference, Glendon College, York University, Toronto, Canada.

Gambetti, A. & Gandini, L. (2006, October 20). Opening conference sessions at the Hundred Languages of Children Exhibit, Toronto, Canada.

Gandini, L. (1993). The fundamentals of the Reggio Emilia approach to early childhood education, *Young Children, 49*(1), 4–8.

Gardner, H. (1999). *Intelligence reframed: Multiple intelligences for the 21st century*. New York: Basic.

Giudici, C., Rinaldi, C., & Krechevsky, M. (Eds.). (2001). *Making learning visible: Children as individual and group learners*. Cambridge, MA: Project Zero; and Reggio Emilia, Italy: Reggio Children.

Heshusius, L. (1994). Freeing ourselves from objectivity: Managing subjectivity or turning toward a participatory mode of consciousness? *Educational Researcher, 23*(2), pp. 15–22.

Jones, E., Evans, K., & Rencken, K. (2001). *The lively kindergarten*. Washington, DC: National Association for the Education of Young Children.

Jones, E. & Nimmo, J. (1994). *Emergent curriculum*. Washington, DC: National Association for the Education of Young Children.

Katz, L. (1998). What can we learn from Reggio Emilia? In C. Edwards, L. Gandini, & G. Forman (Eds.), *The hundred languages of children: The Reggio Emilia approach—advanced reflections* (pp. 27–45). Greenwich, CT: Ablex.

Katz, L., & Chard, S. (1998). *Issues in selecting topics for projects*. Urbana, IL: ERIC Clearinghouse on Early Education and Parenting. (EDO-PS-98-8)

Katz, L. & Chard, S. (2000). *Engaging children's minds: The project approach* (2nd ed.). Stamford, CT: Ablex.

Mackeracher, D. (2004). Assumptions about adult learners. *Making sense of adult learning.* (2nd ed.). Toronto, Canada: University of Toronto Press.

Malaguzzi, L. (1995.) The "what to do" of the teachers. In *The fountains* (pp. 18–32). Reggio Emilia, Italy: Reggio Children.

Malaguzzi, L. (Ed.). (1996). *The hundred languages of children: Narrative of the possible* [Catalog of the exhibit]. Reggio Emilia, Italy: Reggio Children.

Malaguzzi, L. (1998). History, ideas, and basic philosophy: An interview with Lella Gandini. In C. Edwards, L. Gandini, & G. Forman (Eds.), *The Hundred languages of children: The Reggio Emilia approach—Advanced reflections* (pp. 49–98). Greenwich, CT: Ablex.

Martinello, M. L. (1998). Learning to question for inquiry. *The Educational Forum, 62*(2), 164–171.

McCain, M. & Mustard, F. (1999). *The early years study: Reversing the real brain drain.* Toronto, Canada: Ontario Children's Secretariat.

McCain, M., Mustard, F., & Shanker, S. (2007). *Early years study 2: Putting science into action.* Toronto, Canada: Council for Early Childhood Development.

Ministry of Education and Training. (1997–1998). *The Ontario curriculum: Grades 1-8.* Toronto, Canada: Queen's Printer for the Government of Ontario.

Ministry of Education and Training. (1998a). *The kindergarten program.* Toronto, Canada: Queen's Printer for the Government of Ontario.

Ministry of Education and Training. (1998b). *The Ontario curriculum: Grades 1-8, Social and personal Studies.* Toronto, Canada: Queen's Printer for the Government of Ontario.

Ministry of Education and Training. (1998c). *Science and Technology, Grades 1-8.* Toronto, Canada: Queen's Printer for the Government of Ontario.

Ministry of Education and Training. (2001). *English as a second language and English literacy development.* Toronto, Canada: Queen's Printer for the Government of Ontario.

Myller, R. (1990). *How big is a foot?* New York: Dell.

Norretranders, T. (1998). *The user illusion: Cutting consciousness down to size.* (J. Sydenham, Trans.). New York: Penguin.

Nimmo, J. (1998). The child in community: Constraints from the early childhood lore. In C. Edwards, L. Gandini, & G. Forman (Eds.) *The hundred languages of children: The Reggio Emilia approach—Advanced reflections* (pp. 295–312). Greenwich, CT: Ablex.

Peppe, R. (1986). *The mice and the clockwork bus.* Markham, Ontario, Canada: Puffin Books Performance Press.

Piaget, J. (1971). *The construction of reality in the child* (M. Cook, Trans.). New York: Bantam. (Original work published 1954)

Poerksen, B. (2004). "Truth is what works": Francisco J. Varela on cognitive science, Buddhism, the inseparability of subject and object, and the exaggerations of constructivism. In B. Poerksen (Ed.) *The certainty of uncertainty: Dialogues introducing constructivism.* Exeter, UK: Imprint Academic.

Rankin, B. (1997). Education as collaboration: Learning from and building on Dewey, Vygotsky, and Piaget. In J. Hendrick, (Ed.), *First steps toward teaching the Reggio way* (pp. 70–83). Upper Saddle Creek, NJ: Prentice Hall.

Rankin, B. (1998). Curriculum development in Reggio Emilia: A long-term curriculum project about dinosaurs. In C. Edwards, L. Gandini, & G. Forman (Eds.), *The hundred languages of children: The Reggio Emilia approach—advanced reflections* (pp. 215–237). Greenwich, CT: Ablex Publishing.

Reggio Children. (1994). *Open window.* [Slides]. Reggio Emilia, Italy: Reggio Children.

Rinaldi, C. (1998). Projected curriculum constructed through documentation—Progettazione. In C. Edwards, L. Gandini, & G. Forman (Eds.), *The hundred languages of children: The Reggio Emilia approach 2nd ed.—Advanced Reflections* (pp. 113–125). Westport, CT: Ablex.

Rinaldi, C. (2001). Infant-toddler centers and preschools as places of culture. In C. Giudici, M. Krechevsky, & C. Rinaldi, (Eds.), *Making learning visible: Children as individual and group learners* (pp. 38–46). Cambridge, MA: Project Zero; Reggio Emilia, Italy: Reggio Children.

Rinaldi, C. (2003). The teacher as researcher. *Innovations in Early Education: The International Reggio Exchange, 10*(2), 1–4.

Rinaldi, C. (2006). *In dialogue with Reggio Emilia: Listening, researching and learning.* New York: Routledge.

Rubizzi, L. (2001). Documenting the documenter. In C. Giudici, C. Rinaldi, & M. Krechevsky (Eds.), *Making learning visible: Children as individual and group learners* (pp. 94–115). Cambridge, MA: Project Zero; and Reggio Emilia, Italy: Reggio Children.

Schon, D. (1983). *The reflective practitioner: How professionals think in action.* New York: Basic Books.

Stefoff, R. (1997). *Starfish.* Tarrytown, NY: Benchmark Books.

Topal-Weisman, C., & Gandini, L. (1999). *Beautiful stuff: Learning with found materials.* St. Paul, MN: Redleaf Press.

Trungpa, Chogyam. (1987). *Shambhala: The sacred path of the warrior.* Boston: Shambhala Publications.

Van Camp, R. (2003). *What's the most beautiful thing you know about horses?* (G. Littlechild, Illus.) Edmonton, Canada: Pub Group West.

Van de Walle, J. (2001). *Elementary and middle school mathematics: Teaching developmentally* (4th Ed.). New York: Pearson Longman.

Vecchi, V. (Ed.). (2001). *A rustling of wings: Children's theories about angels.* Reggio Emilia, Italy: Reggio Children.

Vecchi, V. (Ed.). (2002). *Theater curtain: The ring of transformations.* Reggio Emilia, Italy: Reggio Children.

Vecchi, V. & Giudici, C. (Eds.).(2004). *Children, art, artists: The expressive languages of children, the artistic language of Alberto Burri.* Reggio Emilia, Italy: Reggio Children.

Vygotsky, L. S. (1978). *Mind in society: The development of higher psychological processes.* Cambridge, MA: Harvard University Press.

Wallas, G. (1926). *The art of thought.* New York: Harcourt.

Whittin, D. J., & Whittin, P. E. (1996). Inquiry at the window: The year of the birds. *Language Arts, 73*(2), 82–88.

Wien, C.A. (1994). *"Developmentally appropriate practice in 'real life'": Stories of teacher practical knowledge.* New York: Teachers College Press.

Wien, C.A. (1997). A Canadian in Reggio Emilia: The 1997 study tour. *Canadian Children, 22*(2), 30–38.

Wien, C.A. (2000). A Canadian interpretation of Reggio Emilia: Fraser's provocation. *Canadian Children, 25*(1), 20–27.

Wien, C.A. (2004a). From policing to participation: Overturning the rules and creating amiable classrooms. *Young Children, 59*(1), 34-40.

Wien, C. A. (2004b). *Negotiating standards in the primary classroom: The teacher's dilemma.* New York: Teachers College Press.

Wien, C.A. (2006, Spring). Emergent curriculum. *Connections* (Child Care Connections, Halifax, Nova Scotia, Canada), *10*(1).

Wien, C.A., & Callaghan, K. (2007). "Fragile moments": Artists coconstructing creative experience with children, parents, and early childhood educators. *Innovations in Early Education: The International Reggio Exchange, 14*(2), 13–21.

Wien, C. A., Keating, B. L., & Coates, A. (in press). Moving into uncertainty: Sculpture with 3–5 year-olds. *Young Children.*

Wiggins, G., & McTighe, J. (1998). *Understanding by design.* Alexandria, VA: Association for Supervision and Curriculum Development.

Will, D. (2007). *"Can we talk questions?" Imagination and inquiry in young children.* Unpublished masters thesis, Faculty of Education, York University, Toronto, Canada.

Williams, K. L. (1990*). Galimoto.* New York: Lothrop, Lee & Shepard Books.

Wilson, A. (1983). *Magical thought in creative writing: The distinctive roles of fantasy and imagination in fiction.* South Woodchester, England: Thimble Press.

Zull, J. (2004). The art of changing the brain. *Educational Leadership, 62*(1), 68–72.

About the Contributors

Jennifer Armstrong is principal of the junior school in an independent school for girls that has been studying Reggio-inspired processes. She has an MA in curriculum and applied psychology from the University of Toronto, and taught elementary French immersion. She cochaired the institutional partnership that hosted the Reggio Emilia exhibit "The Hundred Languages of Children" in Toronto.

Vanessa Barnett is an artist educator and early years instructional leader in the Toronto District School Board. She is currently a doctoral student in the Faculty of Education, York University. Her academic interests lie in the field of emergent curriculum and graphic representation.

Noula Berdoussis has been an elementary teacher of Grades 1 to 3, and special education, for 8 years in a large urban board in Toronto. She has an MEd from York University and her thesis focused on Reggio-inspired emergent curriculum.

Deborah Halls is a kindergarten teacher in Toronto working on her MEd at York University. For many years she worked as an educational intervener, advocating for and highlighting the strengths of children at risk. She was first inspired by the Reggio Emilia approach while earning an ECE credential at Seneca College.

Susan Hislop is currently the Grade 1 teacher at an independent school for girls that has been studying Reggio-inspired processes. After training as a teacher in the United Kingdom, Susan spent 10 years teaching in a variety of international schools in Egypt, Cyprus, and Malaysia before settling in Canada 15 years ago.

Brenda Jacobs has taught in Oxford, England as well as Vancouver and Toronto. She taught with the Toronto District School Board for several years and currently teaches Grade 1 at the Mabin School. She has an MEd from York University, where her research focused on emergent curriculum and the Reggio Emilia approach.

Mary Jane Miller is a teacher with the Toronto District School Board. Over the past 20 years, she has taught children from junior kindergarten to Grade 5 in urban public schools. She has an MEd from York University where her thesis focused on Reggio-inspired documentation.

Shaune Palmer, a principal in the public school system, is presently teaching in the preservice teacher education program at York University. She taught for many years in a variety of communities and also served as a special education consultant and language trainer.

Nancy Thomas taught kindergarten through Grade 3 for over 30 years before recently retiring. She spent most of her career in the Peel District School Board working with young children and their families. She continues to be inspired by the educators of Reggio Emilia and looks forward to considering all the possibilities that retirement offers.

Carol Anne Wien teaches in the Faculty of Education, York University, and was thesis supervisor and mentor to many of the contributors in this volume. Her previous books include *Negotiating Standards in the Primary Classroom* and *Developmentally Appropriate Practice in "Real Life."*

Diana Will has been a literacy coordinator, primary teacher, and special education teacher for 11 years. She has worked with teachers and student teachers in developing their literacy programs. She is interested in how children use their imaginations, creativity, and curiosity to learn about their world, which was the topic of her recently completed master of education thesis.

Alice Wong has taught infants, toddlers, and preschool children in centers in Ontario. She has an MA from York University and is currently a doctoral student in early childhood education at the University of Toronto.

Index